# MASTERING SALES LEADERSHIP

## THE ULTIMATE GUIDE TO
## **HIGH-PERFORMING** SALES TEAMS

### stevenjenkins

Published by New Generation Publishing in 2023

Copyright © Steven Jenkins 2023

First Edition

ISBN

Paperback: 978-1-80369-857-1

Ebook: 978-1-80369-863-2

www.newgeneration-publishing.com

FOR MY WIFE
GERALDINE WHO
WHOLEHEARTEDLY
SUPPORTS MY WORK
AND UNDERSTANDS
THAT I CAN NEVER RETIRE!

I COULDN'T DO THIS
WITHOUT YOU.

# CONTENTS

# ACKNOWLEDGEMENTS

Firstly I would like to thank my wife Geraldine for her unceasing support for my work and for being a brilliant and constructive proof-reader. I would like to thank Susie Vincent and her team at Greenwood Solutions for creating the designs, illustrations, and artwork for the book. Also to David Walshaw and his team at New Generation Publishing who have been invaluable in getting the book to market.

I would like to offer huge thanks to the people who have inspired me in my life and helped me along a very varied career to date. To my gifted schoolteacher, Lance Bean who gave me a lifelong passion for language, especially the French language. This has been a key part of my early career and enabled me to become an export manager for the French market in industrial textiles with Turner & Newall. It also enabled me to get the job as Middle East and Africa manager for Van Heusen (Carrington Viyella) where the interview was in French! The experience of seeing these markets was priceless. My huge thanks go to the many amazing people I worked with during my time with MARS. I had some brilliant bosses including Ed Wal and Peter Erskine who both went on to have incredible careers after MARS. I must also acknowledge Nicholas Gartside of the Peter Guy Partnership for his outstanding sales training programmes that provided a firm structure and basis for my sales career. Special thanks must go to my ex-boss David Henderson whom I encouraged to leave MARS and join me in running my direct advertising agency. He is certainly the smartest person I have ever worked with, and he gave me a deep understanding of strategy and planning that has served me well. We worked in a highly productive partnership for over ten years in building SJA into the great agency it became.

Huge thanks also to Marcus Moir who acted for me in the sale of my agency and who has become a great friend. Marcus is credited with getting me into coaching when he asked me to work in a group he was Chairing at the time. In no time I was coaching and mentoring over 20 people in the group. It was a perfect fit for me and showed me that coaching is a great way to use my experience to help managers address their challenges. I would also like to acknowledge the Henley Business School for helping me become an accredited Executive Coach and huge thanks to Claire Pedrick at 3D Coaching for turning me into a confident coach by adopting her Simplified Coaching methods.

I have been inspired by Mike Weinberg, an American Sales guru who has written some powerful books on selling and sales management. His approach and style are very much in synchrony with my own experiences, and I frequently refer to his work in my sales coaching. Also, I acknowledge David Ventura and Phil Jesson whose brilliant book "10 Top Tips for your Ten Top customers" is a regular source of reference when working with Key Account management. Both Mike, David and Phil must owe me a commission for the number of times I have recommended their brilliant books to my coaching clients!

# ABOUT THE AUTHOR

I work at all levels in the organisation but am particularly interested in working at C-Suite/Director level where it is possible to help stimulate change from the top that will have the greatest impact on the organisation

I began my career in academia but quickly realised that this was too narrowly focused. I wanted to change the world!

My corporate life began working with three Blue Chip organisations in sales roles. One of these roles was Export Manager for Van Heusen luxury shirts looking after Africa and the Middle East. However, my formative years were spent as a marketing manager in the MARS Group where I was responsible for building the Klix and Flavia coffee and tea systems into huge global businesses. I worked with amazing people and looked after the UK, Europe, North America, Scandinavia and Middle East markets during my time with the company.

It was at Mars that I was asked to manage a number of sales teams, which was a seminal moment in my career. I learned how to work in a very hands-on way with my salespeople and to help them use their own sales reports as a self-development tool. In addition to receiving fantastic training in speciality sales, need creation, negotiation and management techniques I learned that the only way to run a sales team was at the coal face.

Whilst at Mars I became a specialist in lead generation using direct marketing methods and, after 8 years with the company I left to establish my own Direct Advertising agency. I ran this agency for 15 years and built it up to a £10 million turnover business and the most profitable agency in the market. During my time with the agency, I was responsible for all new business, generating £1 million every year for 15 years.

I won major Blue-Chip clients like Coca-Cola, Schweppes, Toshiba, Commercial Union and Sainsbury's. We had the best client and staff retention in the marketplace. The agency was eventually sold to HAVAS, a global advertising group, and I became Vice-Chairman of the UK company, Brann Worldwide.

Over the last 20 years, I have been involved in two start-up businesses involving me in working at Board level with companies like Nestle and Pepsi-Cola. I have also worked as a consultant helping companies that wanted to grow, become more profitable and exit.

In recent years, I have worked as a business coach and mentor using my 45 years of experience to help managers at all levels to achieve their goals. Sales productivity and business development remain my area of speciality.

**STEVEN JENKINS ACC**
SALES PERFORMANCE COACH

# FOREWORD

I have known Steven for over 40 years. In fact, my very first exposure to Steven was at Mars where he worked for me as a product manager on Klix Drinks (A division of Mars) which was a revolutionary vending machine that tied users to purchasing the consumable range of teas and coffees. His yearning was in the direction of sales and soon progressed into that area inspiring a generation of sales personnel who found his commitment, style and methodology focused and outstanding. After leaving Mars, he became the Founder member of a creative direct marketing agency which was sold for a seven-figure sum in 2000. In that business, his sales skills attracted many international organisations which established the agency as a major player in its marketplace.

I developed my career by creating a business-to-business sales qualification process called STRONGMAN which forces the salesperson to ask uncomfortable questions. When applied with rigour the process can double sales. Steven, in this book concentrates on sales management and its relevance and importance to managing and leading sales teams in a very positive way. His no-nonsense attitude permeates the narrative and generates results when applied by the senior leadership within a company.

In this book Steven brings realism to sales management; it is based on real-life experience which is practical and thoroughly tested. As most of you know there are many courses on Economics, Psychology, Business Leadership and Finance etc but there are few courses on Selling or Sales Leadership. In this book, Steven brings a rare insight into the importance and skills associated with creating a sales culture and environment to grow sales year after year. Sales management is considered instinctive and one famous CEO once said to me "We recruit intelligent people from top universities, and they will figure it out." My response was "Why have you employed a CFO who did a finance degree at a top university followed by 3 years in a Top 4 accounting firm working and studying how to become a CFO". His response was; "Point taken" and from there training, development and the creation of a sales culture started. It never ceases to amaze me that the key document produced by any CFO is the P&L. The very first line is Revenue ie what has been sold!

This is what Steven captures in his book *Mastering Sales Leadership: The Ultimate Guide to High-Performing Sales Teams*", and he makes it very clear that there is no company without the sales team. To build an effective sales team there is a requirement for an organisation to create a sales culture and there is no sales culture without an effective plan or accountability. It never ceases to surprise me that so many organisations do not see any reason to write sales plans. Without plans, there is no purpose, success or failure and if this is all you take from this book, then you will already be more successful.

Sales managers not only create culture but also complete a number of key tasks, usually, one-to-one mentoring, field accompaniment, managing sales plans and their achievement, deal analysis and rehearsing the next steps on a particular sale. It is not chasing non-payment of invoices, checking activity or call rates. Sales managers know they need to manage real opportunities and not activity. It is with genuine sales opportunities that sales managers can add an extra dimension. They can see the direction the salesperson should take or the offer they should make in closing the sale. In order to do that they will need to spend time with the salesperson understanding their opportunities and directing them.

Modern sales managers seem to have an obsession with CRM which is important and requires management, but not to the exclusion of the sales management role which is primarily understanding the team and what motivates them to succeed. Sales managers are so often absorbed with lead conversion statistics, activity levels, pipeline management and averages. I have heard average order values and average meetings booked. These are a waste of sales management effort. If a salesperson achieves averages then they will be average and the business will be average and that is not the objective of the exercise.

In this book, Steven identifies the unpopular actions of sales management. One of these is not accepting poor performance. By doing this there is an acceptance that it is fine to tolerate poor performance when clearly it is not.

Sales management is there to support, mentor and accompany and sometimes this fails particularly in the new acquisition of clients. The moment sales management debates this issue then there is a problem. Sales managers must take the unpopular decision of releasing the poor performer. This adds to the improvement of the sales team and acts as a signal to other team members that not performing has consequences and that the sales manager will not flinch from this task.

As I said in my opening paragraph, I have known Steven for over 40 years and he has brought a wealth of experience and importantly documented it so that others can learn. In his consultancies, he advocates improvement in sales performance through a responsible attitude to the development of a focused sales culture where everyone in the team is accountable for sales results. Growth endorses culture and performance and this becomes circular.

In this foreword, I have itemised a few hard learning points but there are so many valuable sales management guides in this book that will, without doubt, help direct you in creating success and a high-growth sales operation.

**ED WAL**
AUTHOR OF **SOLUTION SELLING. THE STRONGMAN PROCESS.**

# INTRODUCTION

## WHY AM I WRITING THIS BOOK?

I have been working in sales and marketing roles for over 45 years now. I have worked in Blue Chip corporations and founded three start-up companies and sold two of them. I have worked as a consultant helping companies who want to grow, raise funding or exit. And now, instead of playing golf and putting my feet up, I find myself unable to stop. I have too much energy to retire and too much experience that I want to share.

Entirely by accident, a friend of mine who was the Chairman of a private equity-owned group of companies contacted me several years ago and asked me to become a sales and marketing advisor to the group's main board and to coach a couple of senior sales managers. Within a few months, I was coaching and mentoring over 20 individuals from Managing Directors to salespeople. I absolutely loved it and found that all my experience was incredibly valuable in helping managers and salespeople to grow and develop their skills. This was the perfect niche for someone at my stage in life who did not want to stop learning and engaging with others in a meaningful and valuable way. I decided to become a coach and took my Executive Coaching Certificate with the Henley Business School and began to build my coaching business. I now have a diverse client portfolio and get huge pleasure in helping directors and managers overcome obstacles, develop winning strategies, or simply sharpen up their sales and negotiating skills.

## SO WHY AM I WRITING THIS BOOK?

There are many sales management books available, some of them focus on sales techniques, others on management practice. Many of them are American and have a distinctly American style. Of course, there are amazing American books, but I think there is a role for a book which has a distinctively British style and flavour. More importantly, there are not many books which look at sales management from a broader perspective embracing the role of sales within the corporate structure, the science of writing sales plans which are based upon reality and not simply in the expectation of percentage increases over the previous year. Whilst some books focus on the sales processes of either new business selling or existing or key account management, I see a need to look at sales from both perspectives. New business is the engine of long-term growth and existing account development is the driver of short-term growth. Not many companies that I have worked with understand the dynamics of the two routes to growth. I also believe there is a need to explore performance development and appraisal using the actual activity data generated every day, week or month by the sales team themselves. Whilst there are books which address management skills like running effective sales meetings, I believe a book on effective sales management must address ALL the above areas.

NEW BUSINESS IS THE ENGINE OF LONG-TERM GROWTH AND EXISTING ACCOUNT DEVELOPMENT IS THE DRIVER OF SHORT-TERM GROWTH.

So this book brings together all my experiences of working with many sales organisations, both large and small. Much of my career has been spent helping companies who are struggling to achieve significant year-on-year growth and so, in working with them, I have observed a number of key areas which have a negative impact on sales productivity. These areas come up repeatedly and so this book deals with these typical areas of weakness and shows how to overcome them. The methods and techniques presented in this book really work and have been demonstrated to work over a number of years working with struggling sales teams. It must be remembered that even small improvements in productivity can have a significant impact on the profitability of a company. Just a 1% improvement in sales efficiency will deliver £10,000 in additional revenue for every £1 million of turnover. Many of the changes presented in this book can be achieved without any increase in overheads and so much of this additional revenue will drop to the bottom line.

I am confident that any senior sales manager will achieve dramatic productivity improvements if they address the areas presented in this book. They will preside over a period of meeting and beating realistic sales plans and become a hero on the Board instead of the punching bag at every Board meeting. They will grow in confidence and raise their market worth. They will create more time for themselves by adopting a coaching style of leadership and in so doing, develop the next generation of super managers within the company. They will reduce sales team turnover and save huge amounts in recruitment and exit fees. They will reduce customer churn and overcome the dangers of having too narrow a contact within those key accounts which deliver significant percentages of total revenue.

Most importantly, sales leaders will have the considerable satisfaction of running a well-oiled sales machine which does not drain them mentally and physically and allows them to enjoy a work/life balance in the confidence that their prestige within the company is recognised as well as their market worth and opportunity. It's all here in this book!

So, let me whet your appetite by telling you what this book will cover...

## DOES YOUR COMPANY HAVE A SALES-FRIENDLY CULTURE?

Be very careful to ensure that your company does not have an anti-sales culture since this has a very damaging impact on sales morale. What do I mean by an anti-sales culture? Well, people in organisations tend to be jealous of salespeople. They think that selling is easy and glamorous and that salespeople make too much money. However, given the option, they would not want to take that job on themselves! I often hear manufacturing managers complaining that the salespeople ask for too many changes to standard sales products or for test or trial products. I hear accounts departments moaning that the salespeople are not chasing payments and invoices. The senior leadership team needs to ensure that the company recognises that without the sales department, there is no company and that all department heads need to sign up for a pro-sales culture and approach. Selling is not easy. It requires energy and mental resilience and if the salespeople do not feel motivated and supported this can impact motivation and can damage the sales results. As Mike Weinberg observes in his brilliant book Sales Management. Simplified [1] it is possible for someone in manufacturing to do their job if they are not feeling motivated. It is possible for an accountant to deliver the accounts if they are not feeling motivated. But it can be very difficult for a salesperson to beat their target if they are not feeling motivated and supported. A positive sales culture is vital if you want to create a high-performance sales team. Instead of moaning about the salespeople, ensure that manufacturing managers ask the salesperson why these different requests are being made and how they can help and how they can support and explore with them alternative ways of meeting their requirements.

## LET'S NOW LOOK AT LEADERSHIP CULTURE

This frankly starts at the top of the organisation. For any sales operation to work effectively salespeople need to be given extremely clear goals and targets for new business. There needs to be a total focus on results and performance, and companies must make sales results highly visible across the business. Salespeople should be managed by their results and not by their activity. In my early career at Mars, I worked for a vending company which marketed the KLIX in-cup vending system. The sales team were charged with building the largest possible base of vending machines which had a tied cup and ingredient supply which would eventually become the main driver of profit for the company. In the early years of the business, the focus was 100% on building the base of vending machines. The company invested heavily in sales training and everyone in the business was very aware of the actual sales performance of each individual in each sales team and each region. The culture of the business was totally geared toward supporting the sales effort. The company was extremely successful and enjoyed considerable sales growth year on year and much of this growth came from the total focus on sales and results which came from the very top of the organisation. I learned a great deal about selling in the Mars Group and I'm extremely fortunate that my 8-year career in the company was spent in a company with such a resolute focus on sales and supporting the sales effort. I should say that, sadly, I have never seen such a culture since!

## SALES PLANS WHICH ARE NOT BASED ON REALITY

I have seen so many sales plans which have been constructed based upon a simple extrapolation of the previous year's performance or, where the shareholders or investors have demanded a growth plan which is not based upon any real analysis of the historical sales productivity. This is a common observation in companies I have worked with and the sad thing is that the plan condemns the sales leadership to a year of missed plans and unnecessary pressure. In the book I explain how to plan effectively, taking into account the potential for growth from the new business team as well as the account management team. I will demonstrate that new business is the engine of long-term growth and key account management is the driver of short-term growth. I will show how consideration must be given to customer churn in planning. The end result is the creation of a sales plan which is achievable and deliverable. In so doing sales directors can enjoy a year of meeting plans and being the hero in the Boardroom!

## SALES MANAGERS NEED TO SPEND 100% OF THEIR TIME MANAGING SALES!

In many companies that I have worked with, sales managers seem to be doing everything but managing sales. Sales managers are frequently expected to chase deliveries, chase unpaid invoices, arrange installations and become involved with innumerable management initiatives. All of this takes them away from what I consider to be their primary responsibility, which is managing the salespeople that report to them, and coaching and mentoring their people to become efficient and effective salespeople. Look at your own sales managers and find out on any particular day how much of their time is spent on activities which take them away from their primary role. Ask yourself how much time they spend in the field observing their salespeople (if they are a field-based operation) or sitting side by side with them whilst they are making sales calls (if they are office-based). How much time do managers spend with each salesperson going through pipeline reviews? How many one-to-one sales reviews do they have with their people? I think you will be surprised when you conduct such a survey. Sales managers have one role and one role only and

SALES MANAGERS ARE FREQUENTLY EXPECTED TO CHASE DELIVERIES, CHASE UNPAID INVOICES, ARRANGE INSTALLATIONS AND BECOME INVOLVED WITH INNUMERABLE MANAGEMENT INITIATIVES.

SALES MANAGERS HAVE ONE ROLE AND ONE ROLE ONLY AND THAT IS TO MANAGE THE TALENT THAT REPORTS TO THEM.

that is to manage the talent that reports to them, recruit quality people, weed out poor performers and train, coach, mentor and support their team at all times. Managers should ensure that their salespeople know exactly what is expected of them and there should be a total focus on results and performance. This is not possible when sales managers are pulled away from this role by the company to undertake non-sales tasks. I would suggest that one piece of homework you should take from this is to conduct an analysis of each of your sales managers to find out exactly how they are spending their time each day... you will be surprised by what you find!

## DOES YOUR COMPANY HAVE A CUSTOMER RELATIONSHIP MANAGEMENT OR CRM SYSTEM?

Many companies have invested in some form of CRM system. The problem that I see with CRM systems is that they are seen as some form of magic bullet to drive sales performance. I can tell you now that sales managers can easily become CRM-obsessed and CRM managers do not always make great sales leaders. Companies often install CRM systems because they are focused primarily on activity often at the expense of a more important focus on results. Companies can spend a huge amount of money installing a CRM system and take the eye off the sales ball whilst they are populating the system with huge amounts of data. The problem is how that data is used for the benefit of individual salespeople. Used correctly, CRM systems should act as a valuable tool for salespeople to ensure that meetings and appointments and follow-ups are not forgotten and that important information on prospects

23

is captured. Also, the CRM system should be a valuable tool in helping to train and develop salespeople by allowing individual salespeople to use the key ratios from the CRM data to manage their own sales performance. Let me explain, in a consultancy-type selling operation there will be various stages which lead to the sale. The first is the prospecting stage, then the first meeting or discovery meeting, the follow-up meetings leading to quotation and hopefully to the sale itself. By analysing the ratio of these various activities to the actual order the sales manager can help the salesperson identify where their sales performance needs to be fine-tuned. For example, if a salesperson has too many follow-up calls per order, the likelihood is that the fault could be that they are prospecting the wrong people who are never likely to become customers or that they have not created and established a need for the product or that they are not good at asking for the order when a need has been established. All of these areas will be known to the sales manager if they are regularly working with the salesperson in the field. Using the CRM data, the sales managers can help the salespeople to use the analysis to point them to areas for in-field training. When I was running large sales teams at Mars, we did not have CRM systems available to us and I had to rely upon daily weekly and monthly sales reports to manage my salespeople. I quickly realised that these reports were gold dust and at each monthly sales meeting the meeting was followed by one-to-one sessions with each salesperson where I coached each person to explain their sales performance, good or bad, using the key performance indicators from their sales reports. Within a short period of time, I had whole teams of salespeople managing themselves, identifying their training needs and setting targets for field accompaniment based purely on their own sales reporting data. This led to significant improvements in sales performance and in turn, helped to promote the next generation of sales managers using the same management approach.

## OVER-RELIANCE ON EMAIL

Alongside the prevalence of CRM systems is the tendency for managers to rely too heavily on e-mail for their communications with their direct reports. An obsessive tendency to focus on activity levels from the CRM system and communication through e-mail will take the sales manager away from direct observation of their salespeople in the field and this is to be avoided at all costs. Once again e-mail is a tool, and it should not be overused. Salespeople are skilled at people-facing skills so why should sales managers deal with them via e-mail? Mike Weinberg draws a parallel with sports coaches when he asks the question; *"Would a baseball manager manage his team by e-mail?"* Of course not. So make the CRM and email systems work for you and don't let sales managers become a slave to them.

SALESPEOPLE ARE SKILLED AT PEOPLE-FACING SKILLS SO WHY SHOULD SALES MANAGERS DEAL WITH THEM VIA E-MAIL?

WITHIN A SHORT PERIOD OF TIME, I HAD WHOLE TEAMS OF SALESPEOPLE MANAGING THEMSELVES.

## SALES MANAGERS WITH PERSONAL SALES TARGETS

Many companies expect sales managers to also carry their own sales targets. In my opinion this is a counterproductive strategy. From my observations, the very best salespeople are extremely selfish with their time and frankly, there is no place for selfishness in sales managers. Their time should be devoted 100% to improving the performance of their sales teams and not being side-tracked by a focus on achieving their own sales targets. Sales managers win through their people so this should be their total focus. How can they worry about other people's results when they are also focused on their own?

## PUTTING THE RIGHT PEOPLE IN THE RIGHT JOB

Let's now move on to look at how clearly defined are your various sales functions and to what extent you are putting the right people in the right sales role. Natural new business salespeople are a special breed. They are natural hunters. Furthermore, they are few and far between. Most salespeople are primarily farmers, in other words, account managers and engineers, in

SALES MANAGERS WIN THROUGH THEIR PEOPLE SO THIS SHOULD BE THEIR TOTAL FOCUS. HOW CAN THEY WORRY ABOUT OTHER PEOPLE'S RESULTS WHEN THEY ARE ALSO FOCUSED ON THEIR OWN?

NATURAL NEW BUSINESS SALESPEOPLE ARE A SPECIAL BREED. THEY ARE NATURAL HUNTERS.

effect, product and service experts. Many companies put these farmers into new business roles or give them joint sales roles and this rarely works. New business requires a hunting instinct, resilience and the ability to handle rejection. Hunters are able to accept and manage this. It is absolutely vital that you very clearly separate new business functions from existing account salespeople. They require fundamentally different personalities and skills, and your recruitment processes must be designed to ensure that you appoint the right people for these roles. It is extremely important that sales managers have very clear and precise definitions of the target markets for their products and provide full training to salespeople on the value proposition of their products and coach them to deliver an effective sales pitch. Sales training programmes need to be put in place to ensure that new business salespeople are skilled at active listening, need creation and conducting effective research. Great salespeople are great listeners and understand the difference between being on transmit and receive modes!

When it comes to existing account management there may well be two quite different roles depending on the value of the existing account. It is not unusual to find that a Pareto Principle exists where 80% of your revenue comes from only 20% of your clients which means that you really do need to put maximum focus on managing, developing, and retaining your important clients and customers. Very few companies invest time in the specialist training of key account managers and a later section in this book deals exclusively with key account management. Key account managers need to be given very clear targets and goals on retention, development, broadening the purchasing base, increasing revenues, and building a partnership relationship with key customers. Ventura and Jesson have developed this partnership concept into a set of working tools in their excellent book "Top 10 Tips for your Top 10 Customers"(2). Companies that fail to do this run the risk of sizeable losses when a key account customer suddenly disappears because not enough time has been spent on managing that relationship effectively. Once again, the people skills involved in existing account development are very different from those involved in opening new accounts, So first of all do not mix roles having the same people doing both new business and existing accounts, and make sure that the right people with the right skill sets are appointed for the new business and customer development roles.

## VERY FEW SALES MANAGERS ARE TOUGH ENOUGH TO QUICKLY REMOVE POOR PERFORMERS

Salespeople are brilliant at providing excuses for not having achieved their sales targets and so often sales managers get lulled into accepting these excuses about how tough the market is and why someone who was guaranteed to place the order didn't for some reason. Again managers who are focused on activity get blinded by the number of calls and appointments made but fail to recognise that the only key measure of performance is actual sales. As mentioned previously, companies must be very transparent in publishing detailed sales reports. Once a

FAILURE TO REMOVE POOR PERFORMERS SENDS A TERRIBLE SIGNAL TO THE REST OF THE SALES TEAM THAT POOR PERFORMANCE IS ACCEPTABLE. IT ISN'T UNDER ANY CIRCUMSTANCES.

A TOTAL FOCUS ON RESULTS IS AN ESSENTIAL PREREQUISITE FOR A HIGH-PERFORMANCE SALES TEAM.

salesperson's probationary period has been met, sales managers must make it very clear that should a salesperson fail to meet their target they have a very limited period of time to achieve target before they will be moved into an exit process. Good sales managers need to be constantly recruiting and ensuring that they have great people available to slot into places where salespeople have either left or are being exited for poor performance. It has been my observation that salespeople who do not meet their target within their probationary period usually around three to six months are very unlikely to do so. If the sales manager has been providing them with all the resource and guidance but they still fail to achieve their target, there is no room for complacency and softness in this area. Failure to remove poor performers sends a terrible signal to the rest of the sales team that poor performance is acceptable. It isn't under any circumstances. Having said this full credit must be given to every salesperson who meets or beats their sales targets. Managers should ensure that each salesperson writes their own detailed sales plan and provides monthly forecasts. Each month, at their one-to-one sales meetings, sales managers should expect each salesperson to report fully against their personal sales plans and performance against forecast. A total focus on results is an essential prerequisite for a high-performance sales team.  Once again sales managers need to remind salespeople that they are not paid to be busy but to produce results. The livelihood of everyone in the company depends on the success of the sales function.

## DOES THE COMMISSION PLAN MOTIVATE?

I have seen many companies create commission plans which fail to motivate the salesforce which seems a contradiction in purpose. The commission plan must ensure that high performers should significantly out-earn underperformers. There is no room for middle-of-the-road pay plans where great performance is not highly rewarded. Considerable thought needs to be given to pay plans which are geared to specific products. If salespeople are rewarded more generously for selling particular products, then don't be surprised if that's where the focus of sales results. Generally, I prefer to see pay plans geared to revenue and margin generation since it is margin which covers the cost of the salespeople in the first place. The pay plans need to reflect the strategy of the business.  Let me give you an example from my own experience by going back to the vending business at Mars

GENERALLY, I PREFER TO SEE PAY PLANS GEARED TO REVENUE AND MARGIN GENERATION SINCE IT IS MARGIN WHICH COVERS THE COST OF THE SALESPEOPLE IN THE FIRST PLACE.

that I worked with in the early part of my career. The KLIX in-cup vending system required the creation of a large vending machine base from which there would be a recurring volume from the tied cup and ingredient supply. The strategy, therefore, was to place vending machines on sites with high potential drinks throughput. Pay plans that were developed around vending machine models failed to achieve this and ultimately the pay plans were modified to pay greater commissions on high-volume throughput sites than on specific machine models. Care should also be taken when creating pay plans which provide a flow of commission to salespeople which is not based upon actual sales generated in any period of time. For example, ongoing revenue from existing customers, because this tends to make salespeople complacent. It also emphasises the need to separate new business from customer management.

## SALES MANAGERS NEED TO LEARN TO COACH AND MENTOR

I'd like to come back to the specific roles of sales managers in the way they should be coaching and mentoring and developing their salespeople. Sales managers should spend time with every salesperson in their field selling environment, coaching and mentoring and developing their sales skills. From my experience, not enough time is spent doing this and at the same time, buyers are more specialised. Procurement departments are now commonplace and so buyers are often becoming better trained than sellers. Additionally, the Internet provides buyers with information that salespeople used to provide so the role of a salesperson is changing. There has never been a more important time to develop the skills of active listening, discovery, need creation and closing  In a marketplace where buyers are becoming more powerful,  sales managers need to spend time in the field helping the salespeople prepare for each call and reviewing performance after each call whilst not getting involved in the call itself. These are valuable sales and life skills that must be continuous.

## SUMMARY...

So these are some of the reasons why companies fail to achieve the highest performance in terms of sales productivity from their sales efforts.  I am sure that if you look closely at your own organisation, you will find some if not all of these issues exist. Take time now and see how many of these mistakes you can recognise in your own business.

Let's just run through the checklist of reasons for failing to achieve full productivity...

- Sales Directors writing sales plans which are not based on reality and condemn themselves to failure

- There's a lack of focus on results and sales targets

- Sales managers are not publishing sales performance reports and reviewing performance with every member of the sales team every month

- Giving sales managers jobs which are not directly related to their job of managing salespeople.

- Sales managers hiding behind email and CRM systems

- Sales managers being obsessed with activity and not with the all-important sales results

- Getting sales managers to carry their own sales targets

- Having the same salespeople responsible for new business and existing accounts

- Sales managers failing to remove poor performers quickly enough

- Poor commission plans which are counterproductive

- An anti-sales culture in the organisation, salespeople feeling unappreciated

- Sales managers not spending time every month in the field coaching and mentoring their salespeople.

- Salespeople not being provided with powerful Value Propositions or trained to deliver a compelling sales story.

If these factors resonate with you, then you have taken the right step in buying this book. You can look forward to receiving detailed ideas as to how to address some or all of these factors and achieving a high-performing sales team which meets or beats the sales plans every month.

Let's start the journey...

[1] Weinberg M, (2016) Sales Management. Simplified Published by HarperCollins Leadership

[2] Ventura D & Jesson P (2019) Top 10 Tips For Your Top 10 Customers New Generation Publishing First Edition; ISBN: 978-1-78955-438-0

# PART ONE:
## BUILDING A PLATFORM FOR GROWTH

# INTRODUCTION

## CORPORATE CULTURE AND PLANNING

Culture matters and directly impacts sales productivity. The foundation stone upon which a high-performance sales team is built comes from developing a supportive and pro-sales business culture. The senior leadership team must understand that without sales, there is no company and so aligning all the functions in the business to support the sales effort is vital. This change must come from the top.

The sales planning process establishes a base for accurately assessing current sales productivity. Without a properly constructed sales plan, how can a Sales Director know if the sales productivity is optimal or not? I have seen very few companies write sales plans based not only on the requirements of the shareholders but based on a forensic analysis of the marketplace and the historical performance of the sales team.

A carefully produced sales plan will allow the Sales Director to fight for a plan which is likely to be achieved and which can be beaten. It enables the whole sales team to work toward targets which are realistic and achievable. Meeting and beating monthly and quarterly sales targets creates a positive and motivating environment within the whole business. Unfortunately, too many companies are forced into accepting unrealistic plans which condemn the sales team to negative pressure throughout the year. Hardly the right environment to retain and recruit great salespeople.

Therefore, creating a pro-sales culture and writing realistic and achievable sales plans will provide a platform within which the sales leadership can focus on improving the overall efficiency of sales management which will drive sales productivity to optimal levels.

## CONTENTS

# 1.1 FROM START-UP TO SMS! HOW DOES COMPANY CULTURE DEVELOP OVER TIME?

This book is all about helping companies improve their sales productivity. To be of value the book needs to address all types and sizes of business. Clearly, one size does not fit all. I was tempted to focus on SME's or small and medium-sized enterprises, since these represent a significant proportion of businesses in the UK and Europe. However on further investigation, I discovered that SME's actually represent 99% of all businesses in the EU! A small business is defined as having up to 50 people and up to £10 million turnover. A medium-sized business is defined as having up to 250 employees and up to £50 million revenue. Having seen these statistics the only thing I can say is that writing a sales productivity book for SME's pretty well covers the entire market! It's tempting to think that such a broad definition is pretty useless if it represents the vast majority of companies. This was certainly one of the many surprises I found in writing this book since I have always felt that my business was focused more towards SME's than start-ups and corporates.

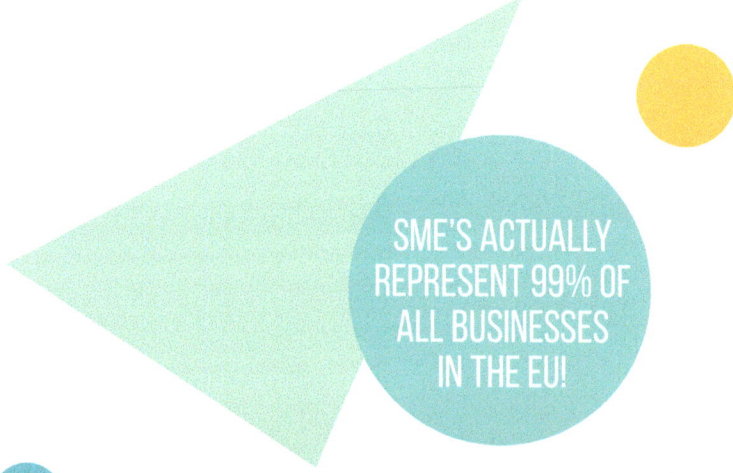

SME'S ACTUALLY REPRESENT 99% OF ALL BUSINESSES IN THE EU!

I have founded several start-up companies and worked as an employee in major corporations. My direct advertising agency worked exclusively with corporate clients and my consultancy and coaching work over the last 20 years has largely focused on SME's. I have therefore observed sales functions across the full spectrum of companies. So what have I learned about the sales strategies of companies across the size and turnover spectrum?

## START UP COMPANIES

If we look first at start-up companies, 20% don't make it past their first year, and a staggering 60% go bust within their first three years. It is well known that cash flow is a business killer, and many potentially successful operations go to the wall because they run out of cash. This is not a corporate finance book, but I would like to pass on my own personal experience of managing cashflow in a start-up business. Firstly I avoided heavy start-up costs by partnering with a supplier company that was a printer and would therefore benefit from much of the work that my direct marketing agency produced. They provided me with an office and a share of secretarial services which made a significant saving in my year one costs. The owner of that business was an extremely astute businessman

IF WE LOOK FIRST AT START-UP COMPANIES, 20% DON'T MAKE IT PAST THEIR FIRST YEAR, AND A STAGGERING 60% GO BUST WITHIN THEIR FIRST THREE YEARS.

who told me to keep a "Little Black Book". For each month I started with my cash in bank figure, and I listed every single cost invoice that came in that month both gross and including VAT figures. On the opposite page I listed every single invoice that I raised including VAT. At the end of each month, I knew what my outgoings were and what my invoiced revenue should be. I ticked off every payment as it was made and every invoice as it was paid. In this way at any time I had a clear idea of what my unencumbered working cash would be and I never lost sight of my VAT liabilities. As my business grew over 15 years, I still kept my little black book even though, with a £10 million turnover, my finance manager kept it up to date for me. Being aware at all times of your unencumbered cash is a highly reassuring thing to have as a business owner.

## BUSINESSES START WITH A "BIG IDEA"

Back to the main subject of this book, where do start-up companies go wrong when it comes to sales productivity? An entrepreneur generally starts a business because they have a big idea that they believe to be highly marketable. The entrepreneur will invariably play the role of managing director and chief salesperson. Early customers will generally come from the existing network of the entrepreneur who will be aware of their specialist skills and likely to buy from them. When it comes to selling outside the entrepreneur's network, the biggest problem the start-up entrepreneur will have is a lack of credibility. In all sales contacts with prospect organisations, there will inevitably come a time when the prospect asks for evidence of the success of the proposition that is being made. At this point, the entrepreneur moves into a 'Catch-22' situation because they have no track record of success and a limited number of clients. Early sales will therefore be made because the prospective organisation buys into the passion of the entrepreneur and the fact that they will be dealing directly with the owner of the business. Generally, this is the way that start-ups get underway by exploiting the existing network and winning new customers through the passion and personal commitment of the owner.

## APPOINTING THE FIRST SALESPERSON

Assuming the entrepreneur is managing the finances of his business effectively, the first hurdle will come when they have no further time capacity to service new customers because the first round of customers demand the owner's personal attention. At this point, the entrepreneur will need to appoint their first salesperson and this represents a very significant challenge for the start-up business. No new salesperson will ever have the passion and commitment as the Founder. Also, the business is unlikely to be able to afford highly experienced salespeople in the early stages. There will therefore be a cash flow issue associated with the recruitment costs and the time it will take for the new sales recruit to cover their direct costs and contribute to the overheads of the business. What I have seen so often is that early sales recruits fail because they did not possess the right sales skills and were not effectively managed. This would result in a repeat cycle of removal of the failed salesperson and the recruitment costs and probationary period of the replacement.

IT IS AMAZING HOW DIFFICULT COMPANIES FIND IT TO DISTIL THE ESSENCE OF WHAT THEY DO INTO A POWERFUL SALES STORY.

## UNDERSTAND YOUR VALUE PROPOSITION

At this point I will introduce one of the most important aspects of effective selling... the powerful sales story. This is also known as the value proposition or the elevator pitch. In other words, what do you do, who do you do it for, what is the benefit to the customer and why you are the only company to consider? It is amazing how difficult companies find it to distil the essence of what they do into a powerful sales story. Much of my sales coaching focuses on just this element. Let me give you an example of my own sales story...

*"I am a sales performance coach. Companies call me in when they need to boost their sales. I believe that every company has a sales challenge that I can help improve within 90 days. I have run sales operations in Europe, North America, Africa, and the Middle East. I have also run several start-up businesses. One of which I ran for 15 years and I personally generated £1 million of new revenue every year throughout that time. I have worked with hundreds of companies helping them to increase their sales revenues."*

In this sale story, I address immediately what I am, what I do and who I do it for. I introduce a challenging statement like 'every company has a sales problem' which is both true and memorable and I indicate that I work quickly because people want quick results. The final step is the reassurance that you have the experience to back up your claims. This is a good example of an effective sales story.

When I started my direct marketing agency, I had a quality business network that provided me with my first clients. These clients knew me and knew what my skills were and were willing to invest in my services. However, when it came to prospecting outside my network I hit the Catch-22 challenge that I mentioned earlier. To overcome the credibility challenge I focused on my sales story which was as follows...

*"I have worked as a client on your side of the desk. I have managed agencies and my experience has been that agencies typically send junior people to deal with the customer-facing role and the experienced people remain back in the office. What this means is that in addition to your existing span of control you have to manage the agency as well. We believe that when you bring in a specialist skill, your job should be to present your challenge and expect the agency to respond quickly with an effective solution. It should not be your job to write a brief for a junior. In our business, you will only see an experienced specialist who can add value at every interaction."*

This value proposition served my agency extremely well for 15 years and resulted in the acquisition of major blue-chip organisations like Coca-Cola, Toshiba, Sainsbury's, Commercial Union and other great clients. Furthermore, by delivering on the value proposition the agency had enviable customer retention and grew to be the most profitable direct marketing agency in the country. It was ultimately bought by a global advertising agency group.

So in a start-up, appointing the first salesperson represents a significant investment but the risks will be mitigated by training them with the sales story and making sure, by accompanying them in their early sales efforts, that they are delivering the message powerfully and effectively.

The next reason why I believe early investment in salespeople fails is due to a lack of focus on results and the acceptance of excuses for lack of sales. From experience, salespeople are brilliant at telling you all the reasons why they have not achieved but always explaining that the sales will follow in the next month.

The effective entrepreneur will set out very clear goals and guidelines against which the salesperson will be measured and there will be an agreed probationary period for them to meet these targets. These targets should be constructed on a reasonable expectation based upon the experience of the entrepreneur themselves. By the end of the probationary period, the salesperson must be achieving a sales margin which covers not only their direct costs but a contribution towards profits. In my agency, I had a simple model that all salespeople had to deliver a 30% contribution over and above their direct costs. The owner-manager should spend quality time every month with the salesperson going through their activity in great detail to ensure they are targeting the right people with budget responsibility and have established both interest and need in the products or services on offer. For every prospect, there should be a clear idea of the budget availability and time scale for conversion. The salesperson should commit to a revenue and margin forecast for the next month and also set out details of their pipeline-building exercise activity. The salesperson should be under no illusion that failure is acceptable and owner-managers will only fool themselves if they allow a salesperson to continue to fail beyond the probationary period.

## AT THE HEART OF SALES MANAGEMENT IS THE SALES PIPELINE

A salesperson needs to constantly recruit prospects who meet the likely requirements for the company at the top of the pipeline funnel and ensure that the pipeline is fully populated right through to sale. There is no alternative for a successful salesperson but to constantly build the pipeline. The owner-manager should be reassured that a perfectly successful business can be built with ordinary salespeople. The gifted sales powerhouses are few and far between and will be too costly to employ in the early stages. Following the basics of training in the sales story and close management of the pipeline with a total focus on results and an unwillingness to accept excuses will give the owner-manager the best chance to grow their business.

If the start-up entrepreneur begins their investment in a sales function in the way I have suggested then, as the company grows there will be a model for further investment in salespeople. As each new salesperson is appointed the company will have greater experience to draw upon in knowing what to look for and how to manage them most effectively.

## MOVING BEYOND THE START UP

A challenge for the entrepreneur will come when they need to take a greater role in the general management of the business and less time client-facing. By building an effective sales operation underneath them they will avoid the problem of the customer expecting always to see the owner of the business, which is the first major hurdle to overcome.

The next stage in the growing operation will be the demarcation between new business prospecting and account management. The two roles are radically different and require very different skill sets and personalities. Combining the roles of winning business and then managing it will reduce sales growth and so the two functions will need to be created to

THE OWNER-MANAGER SHOULD BE REASSURED THAT A PERFECTLY SUCCESSFUL BUSINESS CAN BE BUILT WITH ORDINARY SALESPEOPLE.

maintain the focus on company growth. As the enterprise grows and develops the owner-manager will need to write business plans which take into account that the new business needed to achieve growth must take into account the natural churn of customers. Very few companies take into account that for perfectly normal reasons customers come and go. It is a pretty good rule of thumb to assume that 25 to 30% of new business will simply replace business that is lost for a variety of reasons.

Managing existing customers is an essential skill if the business is to grow. In a later section, I will deal with key account management in greater detail. It is fair to say that the Pareto Principle exists in many businesses where 80% of the revenue comes from only 20% of the customers. Therefore the owner-manager needs to constantly look at the customer base to

A CHALLENGE FOR THE ENTREPRENEUR WILL COME WHEN THEY NEED TO TAKE A GREATER ROLE IN THE GENERAL MANAGEMENT OF THE BUSINESS AND LESS TIME CLIENT-FACING

understand what type of business makes the ideal customer for the enterprise and to seek more like them. Taking customers for granted is a disaster and the owner-manager must ensure that the same rigour that is applied to new business sales is also applied to the management of existing customers. The enterprise should aim to establish a partnership relationship with its clients and constantly explore ways to deepen and widen the relationship in such a way as to become integral to the customer's day-to-day operations. By focusing carefully on both new business acquisition and existing customer management, the company will have the very best opportunity to grow and thrive beyond that critical 3-year horizon.

## 1.2 COMPANY CULTURE AFFECTS SALES PRODUCTIVITY

When it comes to sales productivity the old adage "If you keep on doing what you do then you will keep getting the results you always get". I don't know of many companies who would not wish to increase the volume of sales in their business but very few companies are willing to put themselves under the microscope to see if there are any reasons why they are not achieving their full sales potential. This task normally falls to an external consultant or a sales coach. The problem with this is that the barriers which hold back a company from achieving its optimal level of sales do not always lie in the sales department. Company culture does have a significant impact on the sales team. From experience, very few companies even consider if they have a culture let alone one that may impact the sales department. It's only when you work in a company which has an anti-sales culture or if you are lucky enough, as I was, to work in a company with an amazingly positive sales culture, that you realise just how important it is to have every department in the company aligned behind the sales team.

IF YOU KEEP ON DOING WHAT YOU DO THEN YOU WILL KEEP GETTING THE RESULTS YOU ALWAYS GET.

## WORKING IN AN ANTI-SALES CULTURE

I recently worked with a manufacturing company which had been privately owned until relatively recently before being bought by a private equity business and integrated into a group structure. My role was to work with the Sales Director and his sales team to improve new business acquisitions and also to coach the key account management team. Very quickly it became apparent that there were major problems within this company which were very definitely affecting the sales team and significantly reducing the revenues of the business and some of the company's major accounts were vulnerable. The managing director of the business had been with it for many years and was a sizable shareholder. He was a manufacturing and operations person by background and talking with him revealed strong negative views about the sales team. After working with the business for a period of time it became clear that there was a clear divide between the sales and manufacturing functions which were often working against each other. There were clear areas for management and sales skills development, but it was obvious that without a major change in company culture the full potential for new business and the retention of key customers the company was not going to grow and thrive. The key areas for change lay in the manufacturing function where job costing was being compromised by wasteful practices and there were inadequate controls of production timing and quality control. This resulted in a lower-than-planned margin per job, delays in output and problems in the installation process. To compound the problem, the company relied upon external installation teams who, because they were not part of the operation, lacked the motivation or pride in execution that an in-house function would have. The resulting conflict between the sales department and the manufacturing and operations departments was very demotivating for the key account teams in particular who spent a great deal of time firefighting instead of developing their accounts.

## WORKING IN A PRO-SALES CULTURE

In my early career, I was lucky enough to work for a Mars group company which had an amazingly positive and supportive culture throughout the business. Mars was and probably still is the largest privately owned corporation in the world and the strong guiding principles of the business were apparent in every aspect of its operations. One of these principles was that of mutuality which stated that the company needed its suppliers as much as the suppliers needed the company and the two would work together for mutual benefit. Working for this company was exhilarating. The goals and ambitions for the company were made very clear and rapid growth in sales was the total focus and this impacted every part of the business.

The two manufacturing plants knew that they were totally dependent upon the salesforce and worked extremely hard to meet manufacturing deadlines. There was a strong relationship between the sales and manufacturing management and sales managers were always welcome at the manufacturing plants and were very involved in new product development. The operations function recognised that efficient and timely delivery and installation would lead to high levels of customer satisfaction and create an environment which was conducive to customer retention and development. In such a supportive environment the salesforce of several 100 people was an exciting place to work. Sales results were widely published and everybody in the business knew who the top performers were. Competition between salespeople and sales regions was intense but positive. Salespeople were given regular and very high-quality training in every aspect of sales including sales negotiation and contracting skills. Mars was well known for offering highly paid jobs which, combined with its reputation for excellence, insured that there was always a long waiting list for people wanting to join the sales operation. Everyone in the business was genuinely proud to work for the company and even now some 40 years later there are annual gatherings of ex-Mars people (known as Associates) who always talk with great reverence about what a fantastic company it was to work for.

MY OWN BUSINESS WAS TOTALLY FOCUSED ON GROWTH BASED UPON HIGH LEVELS OF ADDED VALUE AT THE AGENCY / CLIENT INTERFACE.

## BUILDING A COMPANY WITH A PRO-SALES CULTURE FROM THE START

I learned so much during my time at Mars and when I left after eight years with the company to set up my own direct marketing agency, I adopted many of the principles that I had seen at Mars in my own business. The principle of mutuality insured that I always paid our suppliers promptly under their terms of trade and this ensured that whenever we needed our suppliers to go the extra mile, they never let us down. My own business was totally focused on growth based upon high levels of added value at the agency/client interface. All of which where the hallmarks of Mars training. By sticking to these strong principles, I built the UK's most profitable direct marketing agency with extraordinary levels of staff and client retention and the business was purchased by a global advertising group after 15 years of strong and continued sales. I am delighted to know that many of the people who worked for me still meet regularly and regard their experience of working in the agency as the best time in their working life.

## SO CULTURE IS IMPORTANT

Salespeople working in a supportive and positive environment will work to the best of their abilities and any skills training they are offered will have the greatest potential to improve performance. The question you may be asking is why I am raising culture as a factor affecting sales productivity. Can company culture be changed easily? In practice, the fastest return on investment will come from changes made in sales management but if the senior level of the business and the senior leadership team are willing to explore culture change, then there is no doubt that positive changes towards a pro-sales culture can be made quickly.

## CULTURE MATTERS!

As Mike Weinberg [1] observes, senior management needs to understand that without sales there is no company, so it is vital that every part of the business is supportive of the sales effort. I remember back in the 1970s when a company called Video Arts used famous comedians to produce films which highlighted various aspects of business training and culture. Managers were regularly shown these films to improve management skills and behaviour. I remember that one of

AS MIKE WEINBERG [1] OBSERVES, SENIOR MANAGEMENT NEEDS TO UNDERSTAND THAT WITHOUT SALES THERE IS NO COMPANY, SO IT IS VITAL THAT EVERY PART OF THE BUSINESS IS SUPPORTIVE OF THE SALES EFFORT.

these showed an engineer attending a customer's premises to undertake a repair to a product which had been sold to them. The engineer was extremely derogatory about the product, the salesperson and the company and this clearly illustrated just how damaging negative contact with the company at any level can be to the reputation of a business. Non-sales but customer-facing people in the company are actually part of the sales process and so play an extremely valuable part in the sales effort.

## CHALLENGES OF WORKING IN A BAD CULTURE

In my early career, I worked in two major Blue Chip organisations with two very different sales cultures. One of these companies produced high-end branded gentlemen's shirts and I was responsible for sales in Africa and the Middle East where these shirts commanded top prices. In many parts of Africa, one of these shirts would cost the equivalent of a week's salary. I was responsible for travelling to our distributor and dealer outlets throughout the Middle East and Africa. I had to make two selling trips every year to market the two seasonal shirt collections. I was also part of the team that put together the shirt collection and seasonal designs as well as choosing the fabrics that were to be exclusive to the range. The company gave me absolutely no induction into how to sell high-priced fashion shirts or indeed how to take shirting orders and so I arrived at my first port of call in the Middle East totally unprepared. I remember my first call was to a large clothing company in Kuwait City. I arrived at the company in my colonial suit and asked to meet the owner with whom I had an appointment. The owner arrived in full local costume and invited me into his office. I was very surprised that he spoke to me in a cut-glass English accent and in response to my surprise he told me that he had been educated at an English public school and had gone to an Ivy League American University. He told me that his experience with my company had been that the company clearly demonstrated that it did not understand the culture of the Middle East. He asked me to come with him behind the building to his warehouse. In the warehouse he showed me at least half of the 5000 shirts that my company had sent him for the previous season, unopened and unsold. Very surprised I returned to his office where he explained how my company actually operated! He told me that the company would own the exclusive right to an agreed volume of materials for a range of fabric styles from which we would put together the product range for each season. The area managers like me would then go out to the dealer network and sell the range. We would then return to the UK to calculate how many shirts had been ordered for each range and hence how much material would be required. Any material left unsold would be offered to the UK Home Sales key clients like the London Oxford Street stores. My customer then explained that his customers would leave Kuwait City during the extremely hot summer months and would travel to places like London and New York for the duration of the summer. There they would see the shirts that he was selling at a price around £100 at the time, at little more than £10 in Oxford Street. You can therefore understand that my Kuwaiti customer felt that this policy significantly undermined his operation in Kuwait. He said to me that he would propose that at the end of each of my sales trips that I would offer any residual shirts to him at £25 per shirt, significantly more than my company was selling this stock to the UK. I encountered the same experience in each of the Middle Eastern markets that I went to and so at the end of my trip, I went to see the Sales Director and chairman of my company to explain the proposed new strategy, thinking this would be a revelation. I was shocked to be told that this would not be possible as the export department had always sold their unsold material to the UK High Street and no changes were to be considered. I explained to the senior management that such a policy would completely undermine the marketing policy for the Middle East but there was no change to their position. I left the company soon after. This is a good example of a company whose anti-sales culture was destroying a valuable brand. The brand rapidly declined thereafter and has subsequently disappeared as a major global brand.

## THE JOY OF WORKING IN A GREAT CULTURE

Soon after leaving this company, I joined the Mars group working for their vending operation which involved the marketing of the KLIX vending system with its tied cup and ingredients supply. The placement of a vending machine would guarantee a flow of ingredient sales for at least five years.  The culture of this organisation was totally geared to supporting the sales operation in building the largest possible vending machine base as quickly as possible since this would secure a growing base of cup and ingredient supply. Every department of the company supported the sales operation from manufacturing, installation, servicing and accounts being totally dedicated to a smooth sales operation. The company was 100% focused on sales results and everybody knew who the top performers were, and these people were held in very

high regard. Everybody in the company was highly motivated and to this day, 40 years on, many of my ex-Mars colleagues reflect on what a great company this was to work for. I learned so much about sales and marketing from the wonderful training courses that I was put through and the experience has underpinned much of my subsequent career.

I hope the above illustrates just how important a positive and supportive sales culture is to the performance of any business. The sad thing is that since leaving Mars I have only rarely seen a positive sales culture in any company that I have worked with which I suppose may not be that surprising because I am usually called in to work with companies who have sales problems!

## SO WHY IS COMPANY CULTURE IMPORTANT?

Well first of all a positive pro-sales culture will enable the company to attract and more importantly, to retain quality salespeople. Salespeople who work in a positive company culture will sell more simply because the company is prepared to go the extra mile within the business to support the sales effort. A company with a positive sales culture will ensure that delivery deadlines are met even if these are outside of the standard delivery guidelines. One of my clients has an excellent Sales Director and a quality sales team but struggles to meet customers' delivery requirements because the manufacturing side of the business is not willing to make the changes required to increase capacity and provide greater flexibility in production. The senior management team are fully aware that a considerable value of business has been lost due to customers being unwilling to place orders because of extended delivery schedules and yet the production problems persist much to the frustration of the Sales Director and his team. The actual quantum of revenue lost due to poor delivery represents more than 10% of company revenue and this is an excellent illustration of the potential improvements in revenue which can be achieved by changing the company culture.

A COMPANY WITH
A POSITIVE ATTITUDE TO SALES
WILL HAVE SUPPORT FUNCTIONS WHICH
SEND A CLEAR SIGNAL TO THE CUSTOMER
THAT THE COMPANY CARES ABOUT
ITS CUSTOMERS.

A company with a positive attitude to sales will have support functions which send a clear signal to the customer that the company cares about its customers. Great customer service retains business and creates great customer referrals. Bad customer service can often lead to a terrorist attitude amongst the aggrieved customers who will very quickly share their poor experience with others. Salespeople working in a supportive and positive company culture will be happy to bring customers into the business which can be hugely beneficial in terms of business development and customer retention.

## WHAT ARE THE SIGNS TO LOOK FOR IN YOUR COMPANY CULTURE?

- Is the Sales Director on the Board? Is he always coming under pressure for lack of performance?

- Is there a general moan that salespeople get overpaid and mollycoddled?

- Does your Accounts Department constantly moan about the sales team? Do they expect the salespeople or the sales manager to chase invoices?

- Does your Production/Manufacturing Department express frustrations about the sales team? Do they moan that they are always expected to reduce delivery times? Do they always seem to be asking for test products and samples?

- Do the Installations or Delivery departments constantly moan about the lack of information from the sales team making their job difficult?

These are signs that I frequently see in companies that are struggling with sales. The comments are always negative and clearly not supportive. The assumption is always that the salespeople are not doing their job properly. *"Why don't they sell the standard products and stop making everyone's life difficult?"*

So what are the signs of a **positive** sales culture? Ask yourself these questions about your business...

- Firstly is there a positive atmosphere in the sales department and does it feel like a high-performing business?

- Are the salespeople totally focused on targets and results?

- Is there a buzz within the sales department and are great performers celebrated?

- Are sales managers ever-present, fully engaged and leading not just reacting to circumstances?

- Are sales meetings useful and do the sales team look forward to the meetings? Most importantly do salespeople leave those meetings feeling energised, supported, motivated and with new ideas and methods to try out in the field?

- Do members of the sales team feel fully supported, valued and well-led?

- Does the commission plan fit the sales objectives and motivate salespeople to overperform?

- Is there any cap on earnings for significant overperformance?

- How visible is the sales manager? How often are they found working one to one with every sales team member on a very regular basis?

- Is there an intensity and a feeling of healthy competition amongst the sales team?

- Do salespeople feel fully supported by the support functions in the business?

- Do salespeople feel welcomed and supported when they go into other departments within the business, like accounts or production or operations

The obvious question is: *"What can I do to change my company culture? Surely that is a huge job?"*

You might feel unwilling to address changing your company culture in the belief that it is just too difficult. In reality, a company which is failing to meet its sales targets can make significant changes to become a more pro-sales operation.

## HOW ONE COMPANY CHANGED ITS CULTURE

I am reminded of the story of Kwik Fit Euro, the nationwide chain of tyre and battery outlets. At one time they had a reputation for being very customer unfriendly. Driving into one of their outlets was not a pleasant experience. The stores were invariably dirty, cold and unfriendly. The fitters would not engage with customers and wore grubby uniforms. Customers were often obliged to wait lengthy periods of time in cold and unpleasant waiting areas. In terms of the service itself, this was often unhelpful. Women in particular would be told that tyres needed to be changed and batteries needed to be replaced even if there was the possibility of extending their life. They were certainly not female-friendly outlets. The owner, Tom Farmer decided on a radical corporate overhaul to change the entire culture of the organisation. Conferences and roadshows were set up to demonstrate how Kwik Fit outlets could change to make them pleasant and provide a positive customer experience. Staff were provided with smart modern uniforms and were taken through programmes to make them more customer friendly. The outlets were redesigned to provide warm, pleasant and comfortable waiting areas supplied with vending machines. Staff were encouraged to consider if tyres and batteries could have more life rather than just simply stating that they needed to be replaced and this would provide the customer with greater reassurance that Kwik Fit was on their side. The whole relaunch was supported by an excellent TV advertising campaign under the theme, *"You don't get better than a Kwik Fit fitter"*. This complete overhaul of the company's approach to customer service has transformed the customer experience and no doubt the profitability of the Kwik Fit Group.

## CHANGING CULTURE ON A SMALLER SCALE

Kwik Fit is an example of how a major organisation changed its culture. There are many things that can be done on a much smaller scale to promote a more pro-sales culture. However, any such change has to come from the senior leadership of the company or else the initiatives will be unsuccessful.

- An excellent first step is to carry out a "Voice of the Customer exercise". This can be carried out by managers of the company or more effectively by an outside agency that specialises in company relationships and reputation. The idea is to approach a range of customers and ask them about their experience of working with your company. It should be explained that any comments made will be completely confidential and the purpose of the exercise is to ensure that the company is fully aware of how its products and services are perceived at the customer level. Such exercises will reveal whether your company has a pro sales culture. The evidence from such a survey will illustrate problems and issues from all areas which are customer-facing.

- The results and interpretation from the Voice of the Customer exercise should be presented to the board of the company. If the exercise is carried out by an external company, it is likely that the results will not be questioned as much as an internal exercise where the motivations of the investigators may be called into question.

- It will be clear from this presentation which are the problem areas to be addressed. The board should draw up detailed recommendations on how it can change to become far more sales-focused.

- The board should initiate a company presentation setting out the findings of the customer survey and explaining how the current company culture is affecting growth

- The presentation should set out how the company needs to make changes quickly and also explain that there will be monthly reviews on performance to show how quickly things are changing

- Typical changes might include:
  - Getting sales managers and production managers together to discuss the problems they feel exist and exploring ways of overcoming them. Frequently such discussions provide insights which were previously unexplained. For example one of my clients, operating in a highly specialist engineering sector, explained to the production function that in order to win large contracts a great deal of work had to be done in alternative product specifications. This was the reason for regular requests for trial and test products which so irritated the production department. However without these trial and test products, the company would have failed to be competitive in a very tough marketplace
  - Getting sales managers to sit down with managers from the Operations function will frequently identify areas in which the sales team can provide better information to enable operations to work more effectively. The operations function should come to these meetings armed with factual areas of concern affecting the sales function so that these matters can be aired openly and constructively

SO IT IS POSSIBLE TO CHANGE COMPANY CULTURE IF THE BOARD ACCEPTS THE IMPORTANCE OF IT AND IS PREPARED TO ACT SERIOUSLY AND WITH INTENT. POSITIVE CHANGES CAN BE MADE WITHIN MONTHS.

69

- The board, with advice from an external audit company, can construct a basis or framework for measuring the improvement in customer attitudes and improvements in sales culture which can be reported on company-wide on a quarterly basis against targets that are set by the board. It is vital to secure engagement into the culture change across all areas of the company and so full transparency is essential if the project is to be taken seriously. Some reward or bonus company-wide could be agreed upon should targets be met.

So it is possible to change company culture if the board accepts the importance of it and is prepared to act seriously and with intent. Positive changes can be made within 6 to 12 months.

It is fair to say that changing corporate culture is likely to be one of the longer-term changes that senior management can make to improve sales productivity.

[1] *Weinberg M, (2016) Sales management. Simplified Published by HarperCollins Leadership.*

# 1.3 SALES PLANNING: HOW DO YOU WRITE YOUR SALES PLANS?

I take it as read that anyone reading this book will understand the need to have a sales plan. Without one there will be no way to evaluate progress year on year and no basis to plan the required resources and budgets needed to run the sales operation. However, in many of the companies I have worked with I rarely find a sales plan which is constructed realistically and so the senior sales leadership is in danger of writing a sales plan which is overoptimistic and sets them up for a year of missed targets with the accompanying stress and sleepless nights. This section aims to provide a framework within which sales leaders can construct sales plans which are based on historical performance, an understanding of the dynamics of the workplace in which they operate, and reflect the revenue and margin requirements of the shareholders.

Organisations which have been either acquired or invested in by either direct investors or private equity funds will be expected to demonstrate consistent and profitable growth over a three to five-year period. Assuming the investors have undertaken effective due diligence and have belief in both the senior leadership and especially the sales function, then sales targets are likely to be challenging. When the senior leadership of an organisation finds itself answering to new investors, they need to ensure that the sales targets they have signed up for are reasonable and achievable. Nothing creates more tension in a business than one which consistently fails to achieve monthly and quarterly sales targets. It is therefore vital that the sales plan sits within the overall business plan and can be seen to be constructed on the basis of reality and not set to achieve the top end of potential sales as this will tend to put undue pressure on the business. Investors in the due diligence phase will respect a comprehensively constructed sales plan and allow the organisation the ability and potential to achieve and even beat that first year's target. At that point, the investor will be enthusiastic to support continued investment behind further growth.

## IS THE COMPANY CULTURE SUPPORTING SALES?

A good start for the sales plan could be an overview of the company culture with respect to a supportive sales environment. What do I mean by this? The Sales Director should take a critical overview of the challenges within the business which affect the sales function. We have already addressed the importance of company culture. An assessment of this should be incorporated into the sales plan considerations. For example, I have worked with a high-tech company which is in an enviable situation of having a sales function that is delivering significantly above plan revenues and margin but where the factory is unable to manufacture, deliver and achieve the quality standards required. This obviously affects the motivation of the sales team and outsourcing and re-manufacturing substandard products will significantly and negatively impact gross margins. It is a fact that without sales there is no company! For this reason, all the support functions within the business must be geared to support the sales function as effectively as possible. The Sales Director, in constructing the sales plan, should identify where other support functions need to change in order to create a positive environment in which sales productivity can flourish. Let's look at a couple of examples:

- The manufacturing department may need to understand that when operating in a fast-evolving high-tech marketplace, the sales team will often require non-standard samples as part of the process of winning new tenders. Such an understanding between sales and manufacturing will avoid the frustrations of providing non-standard products.

73

- The operations function needs to be fully aware of its role in the sales process and understand that slow delivery and careless installation will have a very negative impact on customer satisfaction. This can be particularly challenging when outsourcing such critical functions as delivery and installation.

By highlighting such issues within the organisation, the Sales Director should consider how closer co-ordination between functions can be managed.

## LET'S NOT IGNORE THE OUTSIDE WORLD!

The next section of the sales plan must present an overview of the marketplace within which the company operates since clearly no company functions in a vacuum. How will the economic situation in the marketplaces in which the company operates impact sales? What are the growth trends within the industry and how well-equipped is the company to meet these new trends? Are there any new regulations coming into effect which may impact the saleability of the company's products? Very importantly there needs to be an assessment of the competitive environment and the effect this may have on sales volumes and margins. A SWOT analysis of the competitors against the company will highlight areas of focus, and a Boston matrix style of product life stage will highlight if the company has a suitably competitive product set. Compiling such a market overview may well involve the Sales Director working closely with the marketing director.

## DON'T IGNORE HISTORY!

Sales plans must take into account the historical performance of the sales team. The plan must forensically understand the source of the previous year's revenues. The company needs to understand how much new business or how many new customers are brought into the business each year and how much business comes from existing customers. This historical examination must identify typical levels of churn, in other words, revenue from the previous year which does not repeat in the following year. There are many reasons why customers leave or do not spend at the same level year after year, and they do not always reflect badly on the organisation. It may just be that a project has been completed. It is of course valuable to know why customers churn and to what extent this is due to competitive inroads. It is not unusual for 25 to 30% of the previous year's revenues not to be achieved in the following year. For this reason, the sales plan needs to factor in the replacement of churn in its annual growth target. Many companies that I have worked with fail to take this into account. Clearly high levels of churn should highlight further research by the Sales Director to see if there are ways in which customer churn can be reduced.

## NEW BUSINESS

New business is the Holy Grail and driver of future growth. It is important that the Sales Director ensures that there is clear demarcation within the sales team of those whose role is exclusively to generate new customers and who are not given account management tasks. The skills required to open new customers are comprehensively different to those of existing account development and companies who combine roles are very likely to reduce their sales productivity. If such roles have historically been combined, it would be useful to understand the actual productivity in terms of the percentage of new business against the percentage of sales from existing customers. Over 45 years of sales experience have reinforced to me the importance of separating new business from account management. Such a decision has dramatic consequences on the recruitment process and this will be addressed later in this book.

The Sales Director needs to understand the average productivity of new business salespeople and calculate the volume of new business which can be achieved with the existing resource. Very importantly, the historical analysis needs to look at revenue and margin flows from new customers. Sales cycles in the business-to-business sector can be quite extended and 6 to 12 months from a first appointment to the ultimate sale is not uncommon. For this reason, the Sales Director will need to plan for new recruits into the new business team in the knowledge that it is likely to take up to three months to train a new recruit to the stage at which they will hit monthly targets. New business growth needs to be very carefully planned and recruitments made early in the year in order to impact that year's revenues.

Indeed when developing a new business strategy, it is absolutely vital that the Sales Director understands where the new business needs to come from in order to generate customers who will deliver above-average revenue and margin and significant lifetime value. Data from the CRM system can be very useful in evaluating customer lifetime value.

# EXISTING CUSTOMER DEVELOPMENT

If new business is the driver of future growth, then the current year's growth is likely to come from existing customer development. The sales plans should comprise an analysis of existing customers in terms of revenue and margin. This should enable the Sales Director to understand the importance of existing customers and consider classifying them into Tiers One, Two and Three. The Pareto Principle, also known as the 80/20 rule frequently demonstrates that up to 20% of the customer base could deliver up to 80% of the revenues. For this reason, the Sales Director will need to ensure that their most effective account managers are assigned to the tier-one customers (key account management strategy will be covered later).

In determining the sales revenue and margins from existing customers, a churn factor will need to be applied as mentioned earlier. The Sales Director will need to assess if the revenue and margin target for the year can be achieved from existing accounts after deducting the revenues and margins from the new business team. It will be important for the Sales Director to take a careful assessment of the performance of the existing accounts team since they will be the key driver of the current year's sales target. The good thing to note here is that changes to the key account strategy are likely to have a much quicker payback than the equivalent strategy changes in the new business area. For this reason, the sales plan will need to ensure that there are adequate account management resource to achieve the desired outcome. Consideration will need to be give to the time scales

for recruitment and training plus the associated costs. Again it is a fact that good account managers are much easier to recruit than good new business people.

## Summary

- Make sure the sales plan addresses both the internal company issues which may affect performance as well as having a clear picture of the marketplace in which the company operates. Conduct careful analysis of the historical sources of revenues and understand the contribution of new business and existing accounts.

- Keep new business and account management roles very separate if you wish to maximise sales productivity

- Recognise that whilst new business is the driver of future revenues, scaling up new business will take time to deliver and may not impact the year one growth target.

- The quickest way to grow revenues is to focus on existing account development. Not only will it develop the fastest return, but better management of customers will also have the benefit of reducing customer churn.

# PART TWO:
## BUILDING A HIGH-PERFORMANCE SALES TEAM

# INTRODUCTION

## BUILDING A HIGH-PERFORMANCE SALES TEAM

So having created a supportive corporate culture and getting the Board and shareholders to accept realistic and achievable sales plans and targets, we can now focus on ways to develop sales leadership skills which will quickly and positively impact sales productivity and create a resilient and stable sales team.

## CONTENTS

# 2.1 LET THE SALES MANAGER DO THEIR JOB

In his excellent book *Sales Management. Simplified* [1], Mike Weinberg raises the valid observation that many companies load sales managers with non-sales jobs, what he calls c**p!... Do you think it would be strange if your finance director started chasing up deliveries? What if the production manager got involved in menu selection in the cafeteria? Or if the managing director decided to run a sales meeting? You may think these are strange questions but in so many companies that I work with the sales manager seems to spend a great deal of their time doing anything but focusing on their sales team. For some reason, organisations seem to think that the sales manager should take an active involvement in various other departments. A client I was working with recently was involved in a root and branch restructuring exercise to overcome a distinctly anti-sales sales culture. There were major issues with the production function of this manufacturing business which were leading to uncontrolled production costs, poor quality control and late deliveries. There were additional problems with the outsourced installation teams. A project team was appointed, and the senior sales manager was a key member. The team meetings took place for several hours every day which meant that the sales manager was losing nearly 50% of the time he would normally have been spending with his new business and account management teams.

IN SO MANY COMPANIES THAT I WORK WITH THE SALES MANAGER SEEMS TO SPEND A GREAT DEAL OF THEIR TIME DOING ANYTHING BUT FOCUSING ON THEIR SALES TEAM.

83

I have no doubt that the project needed input from the sales function, but this could have been provided by the Sales Director with much less time and involvement from the senior sales manager.

Sales managers are frequently tasked with chasing unpaid invoices, chasing late deliveries, and organising and managing installations, none of which is their job. I have said before that without sales there is no company and I believe this to be true. The sales manager is responsible for driving new business and retaining and growing existing accounts. I fail to see that this is anything other than a 100% full-time focus and anything which takes the sales manager away from this primary task will affect this focus.

My formative years in the Mars group were spent in an environment where sales managers spent a great deal of their time out in the marketplace working with their salespeople. In most of the organisations that I now work with, I find the sales managers generally work from their offices. The concept of working in the field seems to have given way to an era of desk management. Managers spend far too much time at their desks analysing the CRM data and managing their people remotely by e-mail and text message and this must be to the detriment of sales growth. In all the companies I work with, I try to re-focus the sales manager's efforts into being more field-based. I do not see how a sales manager can really manage salespeople unless they see how they perform when face-to-face with a customer.

ANYTHING WHICH TAKES THE SALES MANAGER AWAY FROM THESE CORE MANAGERIAL ROLES WILL BE TO THE DETRIMENT OF SALES PRODUCTIVITY... END OF STORY!

Spending valuable time on field accompaniment allows the sales manager to assess an individual's time management, planning, and activity levels as well as their selling skills in front of customers and prospects. Without this first-hand experience, the sales manager will lay themselves open to analysis of sales reports and interpreting the many excuses for failure that typically come with underperformance.

A decent sales manager should be able to manage five new business salespeople and a team of five account managers. This would not be an unreasonable span of control. So let's analyse the time management of such a sales manager. They should be spending a day every month with each of their salespeople so in practice nearly half of the manager's time will be spent out of the office and in the field with each of their salespeople. In addition to this, the sales manager will take a day every month for the monthly sales meeting and the one-to-one reviews with each salesperson in their team. Outside of this core management role, the sales manager will have a number of important functions including order processing, tender documentation, pricing discussions and negotiations in addition to the many other issues and queries that will arise out of the sales activities of 10 people. Anything which takes the sales manager away from these core managerial roles will be to the detriment of sales productivity... end of story!

Having worked in senior sales and marketing roles in the past, I am always surprised to come across managers with the title Sales and Marketing Director. From my experience, the two functions are not compatible within one role which means that neither function will be managed optimally. Sales Directors, like sales managers, should be focused on driving sales productivity. The marketing role embraces a very wide range of responsibilities including market research, product development, pricing and the competitive environment, sales support and lead generation as well as advertising and public relations. I just can not see how one person can combine both roles and yet many companies choose to do so. If a company is serious about maximising its sales potential, then this can only be done by providing the management of sales with a total focus on the job.

[1] *Weinberg M, (2016) Sales management. Simplified Published by HarperCollins Leadership.*

## 2.2 PUT THE RIGHT PEOPLE IN THE RIGHT JOBS!

I have worked with many different companies that wanted to improve their sales productivity and I have been surprised at how many of them had salespeople handling both new business and existing account management roles. I am sure there are examples of where this works really well, possibly in small sales teams where the luxury of separating the roles is not available but I still think it's a bad idea!

This is possibly the one area where significant improvements in productivity can be achieved. Let me explain. Anyone who has worked with successful new business salespeople will understand that they are a breed apart! New business selling not only requires specialist sales skills but an entirely different personality.

Let no one ever tell you that selling to new prospects is easy. The prospecting process can be draining. It's a numbers game and new business salespeople understand that not every telephone call will result in an appointment. It may take 10 calls, even when the call has been 'warmed up' with emails or letters. Most individuals struggle with rejection. Getting nine "Nos" before one "Yes" can be soul-destroying for most people but not the new business specialist. They accept the rejection as entirely normal and believe in the numbers game. They will allocate a specific period of time to do their prospecting and not spend all day doing it. Little and often is their approach. Doing ten calls a day to get one booked and qualified appointment means five new appointments are created each week. Each appointment is an opportunity to sell and an opportunity to ask for other contacts and referrals. That is the new business mindset.

Good new business salespeople do not waste their time. Having made ten prospecting calls to get an appointment, they will not leave it there, they will then qualify the prospect carefully. Once the prospect has agreed to a meeting, the salesperson will set up the meeting time and date at which point the prospect will be completely relaxed. This is the time to ensure they are the correct person to see. A typical qualification conversation could go as follows...

(Salesperson) *"So that's 10 am on Tuesday 3rd March at your offices"*

(Prospect) *"Great, that's in my diary"*

(Salesperson) *"Before I go, can I just check a couple of details with you? If the meeting demonstrates that the product / service is exactly right for you, what would be the decision-making process within your company?"*

(Prospect) *"Well if it is over £5000 then it would need a sign-off by the Managing Director. If it is over £10,000 it will need Board approval"*

(Salesperson) *"I understand. Can I ask what your role in this would be?"*

(Prospect) *"Sure, I would be the Proposer for the purchase"*

(Salesperson) *"Would anyone else need to be involved?"*

(Prospect) *"Yes the IT Director would need to approve the purchase recommendation"*

(Salesperson) *"Would it be possible to involve him in our meeting on Tuesday?"*

(Prospect) *"I'll check with him but I am sure I could get him to join us"*

(Salesperson) *"One final thing, what is the normal time scale for approval?"*

(Prospect) *"Depending upon the value of the purchase, no more than four weeks"*

(Salesperson) *"That's great. Thank you very much. I will look forward to seeing you on Tuesday 3rd at 10am"*

The above dialogue demonstrates how a good new business salesperson ensures that they are dealing with the right person in the purchase process and that they can get any other key influencer in the same meeting, and they also understand the purchasing process and time scales. The appointment is highly qualified, and the prospect will be left with the impression that this is a very professional person coming to meet them. The call will also have made it clear that the purpose of the meeting is to sell.

Natural new business people are like chameleons. They can instinctively determine the approach to be taken with any prospect they meet. They will know that the prospect who sits in a spartan office with few embellishments is the sort who will want to dispense with the preamble and want to get quickly down to business.

Unlike the prospect with certificates and photos on the wall and family pictures on the desk who will appreciate a bit of preamble before the selling starts.

And when the selling process does begin, the good new business salesperson will ask lots of questions designed to understand the problems which created the opportunity for the meeting in the first place. They will explore the impact of the problems and, in so doing, establish a clear NEED for the product or service they are selling. Any presentation they then make will be entirely geared to the product or service and how it overcomes the problem areas and satisfies the need. The presentation will only be as long as it needs to be to achieve that purpose. As soon as the salesperson sees an opportunity they will close the sale. This will generate objections which they will overcome effectively and then close again. This process will go on until the prospect says "Yes".

At this point, the salesperson will establish exactly what the prospect needs to progress the sale. If a formal proposal is required for approval by others the salesperson will make sure they understand exactly what is required in the proposal. Importantly they will ask what the timescale will be once the proposal is with the prospect and will close for a follow-up appointment there and then. History will tell them that once the proposal is with the prospect, it may be difficult to book the next appointment so they will do it in advance.

The purpose of setting out the above selling process is to demonstrate that, whilst the specialist skills can be trained into a salesperson, there are certain characteristics of new business specialists which are not easily trained in. The resilience to accept numerous rejections to get the appointment. The focus on qualifying the meeting. The total focus on establishing NEED before closing the sale. These traits do not come naturally to many people. New business specialists are hard to find. They will also be very aware of their value and will only move for a high-end salary and package. Once you have one of these people, the sales manager will need to understand that their skills cannot be cloned and so getting these sales specialists to train other salespeople will not generally work. Firstly, new business salespeople are rather selfish and they will not appreciate being asked to give up valuable selling time to train others. Secondly, these traits are not easily trained. The astute sales manager will learn to value their highflyers, give them lots of accolades and generally manage them with a light touch and leave them free to deliver their sales targets month in and month out. Managers should put them on a pedestal and give them any sales enquiries that come in.

I hope the above description of new business specialists will illustrate why getting them to manage existing accounts is not very sensible. Getting an appointment with an existing customer is considerably easier than prospecting for a new one. Furthermore, the new business specialist will find it very easy to develop existing accounts which will be to the detriment of opening new customers, the drivers of long-term growth. One challenge in getting new business salespeople to develop existing accounts

THE REALITY IS THAT, TO ACHIEVE FAST GROWTH, SALES DIRECTORS WILL NEED TO UNDERSTAND THAT GROWING THE EXISTING ACCOUNT TEAM WILL DELIVER RESULTS FAR MORE QUICKLY THAN GROWTH THROUGH NEW CUSTOMER ACQUISITION. WHILST NEW CUSTOMER ACQUISITION IS THE ENGINE OF LONG-TERM GROWTH, EXISTING ACCOUNT DEVELOPMENT IS THE DRIVER OF IMMEDIATE GROWTH.

is that they are generally very single-minded and want to close business which can be at the expense of the development of relationships that existing account management requires.

It is a fact that it is considerably easier to recruit existing account salespeople. Managers will be looking for empathetic individuals who enjoy nurturing customers. They need to be very well organised. They will also require good presentation skills. Having found such people, the required development skills can be readily trained into them. The specific skills required will be explained in a later section of this book, but I hope I have explained why putting square pegs into round holes is not a good strategy and the sensible sales manager will always seek a "horses for courses" approach when assigning roles. I don't think it will be necessary here to explain why putting empathetic, people-orientated account managers into new business roles is unlikely to be productive!

The reality is that, to achieve fast growth, Sales Directors will need to understand that growing the existing account team will deliver results far more quickly than growth through new customer acquisition. Whilst new customer acquisition is the engine of long-term growth, existing account development is the driver of immediate growth.

## 2.3 SALES MANAGERS ARE IN FACT TALENT MANAGERS

In Mike Weinberg's excellent book on sales management (*Sales Management. Simplified*) (1) he uses the term "Talent Management" to describe the relationship between the sales manager and the salespeople who are under their guidance. I really like this terminology as it neatly balances the relationship between salesperson and manager and recognises that both bring unique talents to the table. It is also a very positive, respectful, and upbeat description for salespeople. Selling, contrary to the views of many company onlookers, is NOT easy. It requires boundless energy, optimism and resourcefulness and a recognition that a salesperson is only as good as their last monthly performance. During my first field accompaniment with one of my salespeople, the salesman told me bluntly, "It's OK for you Steven, you get your salary whatever happens. I, on the other hand, have to deliver month after month if I am to earn enough to pay the mortgage". This brought selling very close to home and made me realise just what a demanding job it can be, at the mercy of the marketplace.

IN MANY WAYS, THE SALES MANAGER'S JOB IS SIMILAR TO THE ROLE OF A PROFESSIONAL FOOTBALL CLUB MANAGER MANAGING HIS POOL OF TALENTED PLAYERS.

In many ways, the sales manager's job is similar to the role of a professional football club manager managing his pool of talented players. First of all he needs to ensure that he has the right players for the specific roles within the team. Many top clubs with a great squad of players fail to achieve success because they have either a weak attack or a weak defence or indeed a weak midfield. To be successful the manager needs to have strength in all areas of the team. So sales managers need great new business people who are natural hunters with lots of energy and resilience and the ability to take rejection and bounce back. Equally, they need people with great account management and people skills able to maintain, deepen and grow valuable customer relationships. Failure to retain customers puts more pressure on the new business target and reduces the company's revenues. So putting the right people in the right jobs is absolutely vital. Managers who try to combine roles are rarely successful because the skills and personality requirements of the two roles are just so different.

One of the best new business salespeople I ever worked with was ruthless in her sales approach. She was incredibly selfish with her time and would pre-qualify every appointment to ensure that the prospect was genuine and held the budgets and the responsibilities for placing an order and once there she would close the sale as soon as any opportunity arose. Putting this lady in a customer-nurturing role would have been a disaster. Her motivation came from consistently beating her sales target and being a top performer every month. These people are like gold dust they need to be nurtured rewarded and made to feel special.

# RETAINING YOUR TOP PERFORMERS

This rather neatly brings me to the next aspect of managing resources which is retaining top performers. At the top of any sales team, there will be an elite group of top performers who consistently beat target month in and month out. These people are the manager's superstars, and they need to be recognised, praised and rewarded and made to feel loved. They also need quite different one-to-one management. In practise people with these ruthless and successful sales skills work in ways which are often outside of the conventional training programme. Sales managers may well need to adopt a light touch with these people and instead learn from them rather than the other way around. In most cases, a greater return on effort will be achieved by spending more time with other less well-performing people in the sales team.

At the other end of the performance spectrum will be those who are failing to meet their sales target. These will be a mix of new people who are in their probationary period and also those who are out of their probationary period but are consistently not hitting sales targets. Managers must be ruthless with this group, removing consistent failures and underperformers. By maintaining a total focus on results and ignoring excuses whilst ensuring the individuals are fully supported to be successful, there can be no room for persistent failure. Failure to meet target should lead to an exit process.

The remainder of the sales team will be those who are at or around sales target on a monthly basis and these are the people the sales manager needs to spend the most time with coaching and mentoring them in the field to improve their skills whilst maintaining a 100% focus on results.

## CONSTANT RECRUITMENT

This approach to performance management will require the sales manager to be consistently recruiting so that they have people in the system ready to replace those being removed or who leave for other reasons. This must be a continuous focus for the sales manager. In almost every company I work with I find sales managers accepting excuses from salespeople for missing target. Reasons like the customer said they would go ahead this month, but they didn't, or the buyer was sick or on holiday and budgets are not available at this moment. These excuses always come from those who will rarely make it. Sales managers must not accept excuses and focus entirely on results and forecasts. Good sales managers should know the positive and negative aspects of each salesperson's performance and will work with them in the field regularly so excuses should not be acceptable or indeed necessary. In many companies that I work with, there is too much attention given to activity and not enough to results. To return to the football analogy, if a game is lost it's not good enough to show that the work rate on the field was high if the goals are not being scored. There is such a thing as being a "busy fool". Managers must be fair, 100% supportive but ruthless in weeding out consistently poor performance. Taking this approach alone will improve sales productivity.

## WORKING WITH THE TEAM ON A DAILY BASIS

A note of reassurance for you. It is by no means a requirement that the sales manager has to be a great salesperson themselves in order to be a good manager. When I took on my first sales management role, I was not a trained speciality salesperson. However, by focusing on results and developing a simple and effective reporting system and spending time with my salespeople in the field I achieved great results very quickly.

Good sales managers need to spend regular time out in the field with each of their salespeople. It is only by doing this that the manager will be able to observe the salesperson in action, assess their degree of preparation, observe time management and also very importantly, appreciate what is going on in the mind of each salesperson. Selling is a demanding skill and requires a great deal of energy and positivity to achieve the activity levels required. Any problems in the private life of an individual will impact sales performance. Good sales managers have excellent antennae and are often required to be personal counsellors to their salespeople. Selling is a high-pressured career and many salespeople take these pressures home with them. This can cause disharmony especially when the salesperson is not performing well and feels under pressure. A day spent in the field with a salesperson can be very helpful in providing them with reassurance and perspective as well as a professional coach and mentor. Selling is also a people-oriented profession and sales managers cannot rely upon e-mail and telephone calls alone to support their team on an ongoing basis. I'd like to think I have played a supportive role in numerous domestic relationships during my career!

When planning a day of field accompaniment, both sales manager and salesperson need to have clear understanding of exactly what areas the salesperson wishes to work on during their valuable day together. I will come back later to the data that underpins this understanding. The manager needs to agree a time to meet the salesperson on the day which will provide sufficient time to plan the day, and this can be revealing in its own way. I remember vividly a day in which I left my home at 5:30am on a horrible winter's day to travel around the M25 to meet one of my salespeople for field accompaniment. I was due to meet them at 7:30 am and left plenty of time to allow for the notorious traffic on the motorway. I arrived at the meeting point on time and the salesman turned up 30 minutes late despite the fact that his travel time was no more than 20 minutes from his home. This salesman was behind his quarterly targets and when he arrived, I made it very clear that I had rearranged my day due to his late arrival. I told him that I had allowed two hours for my journey and had left very early to pay him the respect of arriving on time and that he had clearly shown no respect for me by arriving late.

I told him that I would be returning to my office and that should he fail to meet target by the end of that month he could expect serious repercussions. Needless to say, that message filtered through the entire sales team, and I never had any late arrivals after that!

At the initial planning meeting for the day the manager should expect the salesperson to provide them with a complete itinerary for the day and have clear objectives for each call and explain the background to each sales call. They should also agree on the specific sales coaching and mentoring requirements for the day. The sales manager should provide the salesperson with a protocol for introducing them to the sales call. In my case, I suggested they introduce me as someone from the head office wishing to see what happens in the real world. Telling a prospect that I was a sales manager would put severe restraints on both parties. I would also agree with the salesperson that under no circumstances would I interfere with the call. Even if the salesperson was making errors, the time to discuss those would be post-call. In this preliminary meeting, I would take great note of the number of calls the salesperson had planned for the day to take a view as to whether this represented an efficient use of time. I would also observe the journey planning to see if they were planning their day in the most time-effective manner. I would also observe the variety of different calls to see if the salesperson had selected a mix of discovery calls, follow-up calls and closing calls. All of these observations are extremely valuable when assessing the performance of a salesperson even before the day has started.

Prior to each call the manager should ask the salesperson for their objectives in the call. I used a mnemonic MIL for this process which is Must Intend and Like. I would ask the salesperson what must be achieved in the call, what is the intention for the call and what would they ideally like to have achieved by the end of the call. This is a discipline I would encourage every sales manager to adopt to ensure that salespeople have very clear ideas as to how to evaluate the outcome of every sales call. At the end of each call, I would ask the salesperson to evaluate the call along these dimensions before offering them any observations of my own. Sales managers should not assume that their observations are 100% correct and should offer their observations for consideration only.

At the conclusion of the day the sales manager and salesperson should compare notes and mutually consider the value of the day and what each party has learned. This is a valuable and joint enterprise and should not be seen as the sales manager showing their brilliance over the salesperson.

## USING THE REPORTING DATA

It is fair to say that field accompaniment should be geared more towards salespeople who are focused on new business. There is clearly a value in field accompaniment for key account managers and this will be covered in a later episode. The new business process follows a very clear progression from research to discovery to quotation to follow-up meetings and hopefully to the sale itself. Every part of this process needs to be captured in the reporting process for each salesperson. In past times this was a paper process but is increasingly now provided online. This reporting process provides extremely valuable data for both the sales manager and the salesperson. In many organisations that I have worked with this sales reporting data is seen as a chore by both parties which is a failure to recognise the valuable information this data provides. When I first took over the management of sales teams, I encouraged each salesperson to analyse the relationships between the various stages in the sales process against their actual sales. Let me explain. A large number of research calls to achieve the first appointment would suggest that the salesperson was not researching the target market accurately. A large number of sales calls per order would indicate that the salesperson was prospecting individuals who did not have budget responsibility or they had not undertaken effective discovery upon which to create need or indeed that they needed to develop better closing skills. Only through field accompaniment can the sales manager know the answers to these questions. During field accompaniment, I would ask the salesperson to analyse their call ratios and identify any reasons why they might be sub-optimal. By focusing on this style of self-management I was able to get all of my salespeople to conduct monthly sales performance appraisals and to set their own individual priorities for their own individual future field accompaniment, coaching and mentoring. I found this to be an extremely effective way of identifying training needs and improving the effectiveness of salespeople in the field. In addition, it helped me to identify and train future sales managers use these data-driven methods.

I hope this section has demonstrated the central role the sales manager has in managing the talent at his disposal. It is only through direct observation that the sales manager will be able to assess the sales and work rate of each person and set training and coaching development plans for their team. In my opinion, there is no substitute for direct observation and sales managers who rely upon e-mail and the telephone and the ubiquitous CRM system to replace direct observation do so at their peril. Even if your salespeople work remotely there is a need for face-to-face observation by the sales manager. Adopting effective talent management methods as described in this episode will have an immediate impact on sales productivity. It will improve sales skills, time management and in-call discipline. It will also reinforce the need to remove consistent poor performers in a timely manner.

[1] *Weinberg M, (2016) Sales Management. Simplified Published by HarperCollins Leadership.*

# 2.4 HOW TO RECRUIT YOUR SALES TEAM

Having looked in detail at the differences between new business hunters and account management nurturers, I am sure you can appreciate that very different recruitment methods are needed to find both types.

So many sales managers put all their faith in recruitment agencies and take the view that when a candidate is put forward that they are likely recruitment material. So often this is very far from the case and the company ends up with an expensive cycle of fee payment (up to 3 months' salary) training and introduction then failure failure resulting in repeated time and cost. At the same time, the clock has been running and it may take six months to get the right person on board.

# RECRUITING NEW BUSINESS SALESPEOPLE

If you accept that new business specialists are a unique breed and, therefore difficult to find, then I think a very different recruitment process needs to be used to find them. By all means, use recruiters to put forward candidates but they need to be working to a very tight brief to specify the type of person you are looking for. I would always run advertisements to widen the net.

The initial recruitment interview can be a minefield. Salespeople are brilliant at selling themselves! I have also found, from experience that failed salespeople are often very good at giving reasons to their old manager as to why they have not hit their sales targets. They can be very persuasive and spin great yarns. Be VERY careful in the initial interview. Obviously, you are looking for individuals who have good interpersonal skills. You want people who have an inner confidence which comes across during the interview. You need to ask them about their previous roles and why they are looking for a change. Especially important is how well they sell themselves to you! Ask them to explain in detail how they would address the first month in the business if you hired them. Look for the questions they ask. Do they challenge you and make you feel you would be lucky to have them? If so this is a good trait.

In all cases, DO NOT offer the job on the first interview. Do get them to see someone else on the same day so you can compare notes but aim to create a pool of candidates who come across well at the first interview and ask them if they would be willing to go into a second and more intense stage in the recruitment process.

In the MARS Group that I worked for, we had recruitment weekends in which a pool of candidates worked with us over the whole weekend. They were subjected to challenges and group exercises designed around the specific roles we were recruiting for. This was a very effective process and gave us the best chance of recruiting well. In practice, unless you are a big name like MARS, you may not be able to get people to give up their weekend but they should be willing to give up a day. You should offer them expenses and a good lunch for giving up their time.

Now you need to construct a really comprehensive programme for the day or weekend programme. Some suggestions for this...

- Give them, in advance, the details of one of the key products or services you will be asking them to sell. Give them the key problems that it/they overcome and the specification for the ideal customer in terms of industry and size.

  - On the day ask them what resources they would use to prospect

  - Set up a prospecting call with one of your existing new business salespeople or a sales manager. See how they go about getting an appointment. Get them to make two calls, one where there will be no positive outcome and the other where they are able to get an appointment. See how they approach this and see if they qualify the prospect when they have achieved an appointment. This will demonstrate an awareness of the qualification process. Also in an interview situation, not being able to get an appointment will test their confidence and resilience.

- Set up a face-to-face sales meeting and see how they handle this. Do they ask questions to flush out the underlying problems that the product or service is designed to overcome? Can they create need? Get the prospect to take a tough line and not make it easy and throw up objections. See how well they have been overcome.

- Get them to have lunch with a couple of existing sales-people and see what questions they ask and get their feedback.

- After these exercises, interview the candidates separately and ask them how they believe they have handled the tasks. Look for genuine self-criticism and explore how they think they could have done better. These are signs of the self-driven hunter determined to be perfect. All good traits.

By the end of these exercises, you should allow candidates to have a break with coffee and biscuits while you take stock of each candidate as a group. I am pretty confident that a clear winner or winners will come through.

If not, don't be despondent, you will have saved a lot of cost and non productive sales time by taking on the wrong person. At this point, you may have a challenge...

- You may have found two strong candidates when you only have space for one. Decide if the business can afford to take on the extra person. If not could you put them in an account management role until a new business role opens up? Alternatively, ask the weaker candidate if they would be willing to be on a waiting list for a short while (on a retainer) until a new position opens up. In a sales team, vacancies frequently arise.

- Interview the winning candidates and make your choice. Interview the star first so that if they do not accept the offer you have a backup.

Such a recruitment process is really effective in finding good new business people. It will give you the best opportunity of making a calculated choice and not be bounced into making an offer on the first interview. Be prepared to pay as much as you can and make the bonus structure very attractive. This will attract the best candidates in the first place. Really good new business salespeople are hard to find and they know their market worth. Make sure the package is attractive! These are the drivers of your company's long-term growth.

# RECRUITING ACCOUNT AND KEY ACCOUNT SALESPEOPLE

In so many ways, recruiting people who will manage your existing customers is far easier than recruiting new business salespeople. However, there are different levels of account managers.

You need to have identified the top tier of customers who can be classified as Key Accounts. These are accounts that represent the Pareto Principle or the 80/20 rule ie 20% of key accounts generate 80% of your revenue. These accounts need to be managed by the very best Key Account Managers (KAM).

KAM's need to possess the following core attributes:

- Personable and strongly empathetic "people persons"
- Naturally well organised
- Have a strategic thinking capability.
- Are creative and able to think on their feet
- Work well in teams

KAM is covered separately in this book but in essence, the KAM needs to be able to develop a key account strategy and plan for every key account they are allocated.

The less capable KAM will work and develop their skills on customers who are less valuable. Over time they can graduate to the top accounts. The reassuring thing here is that key account skills can be trained by sales managers and so a career progression opportunity is available to the sales manager.

Once again the recruitment agencies should be given a very clear brief which defines a KAM and they can use this to draw up a person specification.

Once again, the importance of these roles suggests a two-stage recruitment process. The first stage identifies the best candidates who should be invited back to a second stage interview.

The approach for this second stage should be as follows:

Give a brief of a fictitious customer who should be a large company with multiple departments, brand structures or buying points. Candidates should come to the second stage interview with an account development strategy which sets out clearly the following areas:

- Strategy to develop the customer and deepen the relationship.

- Proposals on how to widen the buying points within the customer and how to use the prime contact to achieve this.

- Ideas to deepen contact within the account.

- Suggest an event to bring together other contacts within the customer and demonstrate how they would manage a team internally to make it happen.

- Ask the candidate what defines a Key Account and prompt them to ask how a partnership relationship can be developed. Ask them what ten characteristics could be used to assess a genuine partnership relationship.

The response to the above interview should clearly identify strong candidates for KAM or for more junior roles. The second interview should involve several people so that a collective view can be taken. If recruitment processes like the ones described are used, then there is a very much greater chance of making a good recruitment and avoiding the costs and time associated with making a poor recruitment choice.

# 2.5 THE IMPORTANCE OF SALES TRAINING

After I left university, I joined the graduate training programme of a large blue-chip industrial company that sponsored me through business school training at Cranfield and Loughborough business schools. The purpose was for us Trainees to decide which area of the business would suit us. After business school I decided that sales would suit my interests and personality and I was assigned to one of the group companies based in Rochdale Lancashire which manufactured industrial fabrics made entirely from asbestos. Yes, asbestos! At the time asbestos was very widely used in every facet of life and my company made motor car brake linings as well as textiles which were made into fire blankets and suits for firemen. As a graduate trainee part of my role was to conduct factory tours for export customers around the vast manufacturing plant. The process started with raw asbestos being crushed before being spun into fibres and then woven into various fabrics in other parts of the factory. Much of the plant in the factory was over 100 years old and I recall with some amusement taking a party of Japanese businessmen around the factory which they seemed to hugely enjoy and spent a great deal of time observing the various manufacturing processes. At the end of the tour, the senior person thanked me profusely for allowing them to see our working museum! They did not realise that our vast factory was actually the real thing!

BEING SUMMONED TO A MANAGER'S OFFICE REQUIRED YOU TO WAIT UNTIL THE GREEN LIGHT SHOWED TO ALLOW YOU TO ENTER. TO SAY THAT THE OFFICE WAS LIKE A CHARLES DICKENS FILM SET WOULD BE QUITE ACCURATE.

I was given the job of assistant export manager for industrial textiles for the French market (because of my French language skills). I worked in a vast open plan and very old-fashioned export office managing a team of six export clerks. We worked at large oak desks which had red and green lights fixed to them. The Chief Clerk, a rather self-important gentleman sat at the front of the office on a raised dais and was able to summon any clerk to his desk by pressing a green light. The managerial offices were based at one end of the export office, and they too had red and green lights above their doors. Being summoned to a manager's office required you to wait until the green light showed to allow you to enter. To say that the office was like a Charles Dickens film set would be quite accurate.

My job was to sell a wide range of industrial textiles to large companies throughout my region for which I was given absolutely no sales training but expected to understand the detailed specifications for the range of products I was marketing. I loved the job and the travel that it involved but I did not see how I would develop my sales skills with such an old-fashioned company. Also, the pay was not great!

HOW TWO MAJOR ORGANISATIONS COULD APPOINT SALES MANAGERS WITHOUT GIVING THEM TRAINING SEEMS EXTRAORDINARY, BUT I BELIEVE NOT UNCOMMON.

SPIN IS AN ACRONYM FOR SUSPECT PROSPECT INTEREST AND NEED.

My second job was with another blue-chip company where I became an export manager for high-end shirts for Africa and the Middle East. I have already mentioned my experience with this company but the point I wanted to make was that once again I was given no sales training at all. How two major organisations could appoint sales managers without giving them training seems extraordinary but, I believe not uncommon. I left this company after my second market visit to Africa and the Middle East because I could see that the company and the brand had no future and I really needed to develop my sales career properly. I needed to find a company that could train me in both sales and marketing.

## AT LAST, A COMPANY THAT OFFERED SALES TRAINING!

It was when I joined the Mars group that my learning curve took off at an extremely steep angle. When I became a sales manager, I was put through a number of very effective sales training programmes run by external training organisations. It was here that I first learned about the sales process and in particular the SPIN sales process created by an organisation called Huthwaite. SPIN is an acronym for Suspect Prospect Interest and Need. We were taught the difference between Push and Pull styles of selling. Push is the old-style door-to-door salesman style of selling in which the salesperson would demonstrate their products and push for the order. Pull selling on the other hand was all about understanding the prospect's business, identifying problems and creating interest in how you could solve their problem and thus establishing a potential NEED for your product or service. This is by far the only way to sell.

The SPIN system identifies firstly the difference between a suspect and a prospect. A suspect is a company or person whom you believe, or suspect may have a need for your product. It is only through the process of discovery that a real or latent need is established. Having established a latent or real need a suspect will only become a prospect if they have Money Authority and Need, the MAN acronym. There is little point in pursuing a prospect who does not have the budget and authority to sign the order. It is only when MAN is agreed that the suspect becomes a prospect.

Ed Wal, in his thoughtful book on sales method, *Solution Selling: The Strongman Process*[1] takes the sales process through all of its constituent stages: Quoting directly from his book...

## Solution

Buyers have problems in business and they look for solutions to these problems. Solutions that are purchased are justified on the basis of business and application reasons but are strongly driven by personal agendas.

## Timescales

A salesperson often has no influence on the timescales involved in a sale and may have to work within those provided. However, they may have a major role to play. The (relevant) chapter looks at how to minimise time wasting and delays and identify when it's right to force timescales.

## Review

Review is an often misused and misinterpreted phase in sales. Salespeople need to accurately define what a review really means and what the process involves.

### Options

Prospects will demonstrate a great deal of interest when exploring options-although this isn't always a buying signal. In many instances, the greatest obstacle to our solution is to do nothing.

### Negotiation

Once a prospect has entered the negotiation phase they have, to all intents and purposes, bought the solution and are now looking for the best financial/service package. A salesperson must be careful not to give away the company's profits.

### Galvanise

Many prospects remain with their existing solution, even though the NEEDS may be apparent to both salesperson and buyer. Galvanising the prospect into action is a crucial sales skill and requires careful probing to establish those areas that prohibit action being taken.

### Money

No purchase can occur unless suitable funds are in place. Prospects often say a quotation is above budget and the salesperson reduces his price or changes the solution. What are the options?

## Authority

In business, there is no such thing as a single decision-maker, irrespective of status. Most decisions involve a number of individuals who could feel the impact of any decision and these individuals invariably make a contribution. While few of them can definitely say yes or sign the paperwork all of them however can influence "NO".

## Need

It is only when needs have been identified and agreed that a purchase can commence.

## PROSPECTING AND QUALIFICATION

The process of identifying prospects from potential suspects must be undertaken before any face-to-face selling can start. This is a vital stage in the selling process and is known as Qualification. A failure to qualify a prospect is one of the main traits I have seen in unsuccessful salespeople. The determined drive to fill a selling day with appointments will often result in poorly qualified meetings. Salespeople frequently express problems or challenges in qualifying a suspect. Firstly because having fixed an appointment they are very reluctant to take any course of action which may lead them to cancel and secondly because they feel

A FAILURE TO QUALIFY A PROSPECT IS ONE OF THE MAIN TRAITS I HAVE SEEN IN UNSUCCESSFUL SALESPEOPLE.

116

uncomfortable asking if a suspect has actual budget authority. In practice, simple sales training will enable a salesperson to first close for an appointment, at which point all the pressure is released. The salesperson can then very politely enquire that should the meeting result in an accepted need for the product or service would the suspect be in a position to sign an order. If the answer is positive, then the appointment can be confirmed. If the answer is negative the next step is to ask for more information on the buying authority and if the suspect could be an influencer in any future purchase. If the suspect has neither authority nor influence, then the astute salesperson should ask who the person with authority **is** and if the suspect would be willing to recommend the salesperson to them and hopefully transfer them straight away. In this way, only qualified prospects should ever be seen by a salesperson. Failure to correctly qualify appointments will dramatically reduce sales productivity. Qualification is therefore a critical part of any sales training programme.

DISCOVERY IS ABSOLUTELY FUNDAMENTAL TO THE NEED CREATION PROCESS.

FAILURE TO CORRECTLY QUALIFY APPOINTMENTS WILL DRAMATICALLY REDUCE SALES PRODUCTIVITY.

## NEED CREATION SKILLS

So having created an appointment with an actual prospect with money, authority and need, a salesperson can then embark upon the key sales process of identifying interest and establishing need. Once again there is no magic formula in this stage of the sales process. Discovery is absolutely fundamental to the need creation process. The first sales appointment should be identified as Discovery and this is where the salesperson will largely be in receive rather than transmit mode. The first stage in the discovery is to learn as much as possible about the prospect company as it relates to potential interest in your product or service. In order to illustrate the discovery process, let me give you an example of how the discovery phase was handled in the vending business. I should tell you in advance that the KLIX hot and cold drinks drink system was being marketed in the UK at a time before the existence of Costa and Starbucks and the UK was largely an instant coffee and tea-drinking nation. Selling a vending system was a very challenging experience because the drinks were at best not as good as making drinks the old-fashioned way with kettle coffee powder or tea bag and fresh milk.

The discovery process in a vending sales call would establish how hot and cold drinks were currently being provided by the company. If the company was using traditional tea and coffee stations, where employees could make their own drinks, the salesman would explore if this created problems for the management. A well-trained salesperson would use problem-orientated questioning along the lines of whether this method resulted in a lot of time wasted, when employees would gather in

the kitchen and spend longer than needed getting a drink. They would also explore the degree to which a tea and coffee station created a mess. The even smarter salesperson would ask if the prospect had any idea how much this provision for hot drinks was costing the organisation when considering ingredients, ingredient wastage and time wasting. The aim of this discovery would be to plant or establish doubt in the mind of the prospect that the existing provision was cost-effective or efficient. If the salesperson identified that the prospect already had a competitive vending system, then at this point the knowledge of competitive products would come into play. At no stage should the salesperson criticise or undermine any competitive product since the prospect might well have made the original purchase decision. Instead, subtle probing questions should be asked that play to the known weaknesses of the competitive system and the strengths of your system.

Any sales induction programme must ensure that the salesperson is thoroughly trained in the features advantages and benefits of their product or service. They must also be comprehensively trained in all the major competitive products or systems. Without such training effective discovery can be hampered.

So having undertaken discovery the salesperson should summarise the findings of discovery in such a way as to establish doubt as to whether the existing provision is adequate and to promote the potential benefits of their system as a potential solution. To follow the vending analogy above, such a summary might go as follows...

*"So what you are saying is that providing tea and coffee for your employees in a kitchen creates a lot of mess and you believe that a lot of time is wasted when people gather in the kitchen for a chat, would that be fair? If you had a fully automated system in which a good quality drink could be obtained very quickly at the push of a button, then would this reduce ingredient wastage and the time taken for an individual to obtain a drink?"*

## OBJECTION HANDLING AND CLOSING THE SALE

At all stages in this summation, the salesperson would seek positive affirmation from the prospect. If the prospect shows a positive reaction to this summation, then the salesperson should move into the next phase of the sales process. If the prospect demonstrates an unwillingness to show they are warming to the alternative, the salesperson will move into the objection-handling phase of the call. Once again in the sales induction process, salespeople should be effectively trained in objection handling. The salesperson will probe for a potential objection and very skilled salespeople will very often push hard to identify an objection knowing that they have an effective way to overcome it. A salesperson must be prepared for lengthy objection handling. One of the unstated objections will come from the fact that people just don't like being sold to! We know from our own experience that when walking into a shop and an enthusiastic shop assistant asks if they can help we will often say *"No thank you I'm just looking*." There is a natural reluctance to be forced into any sales negotiation, that is human nature. Effective salespeople understand this aspect of selling and sometimes will play to it. I was once accompanying a particularly successful salesperson in the field where she had undertaken excellent discovery created interest and established a clear need in the prospect. The prospect then created numerous objections as a barrier to moving forward into a closing phase. The salesperson eventually asked the prospect if he was convinced in his mind that the product was of interest to him. This really forced the issue and required the prospect to say yes or no. In this particular case, the prospect said no not really at which point the salesperson said *"Tell me what I have to do to get this sale across the line and let's identify exactly what the barrier is"*. It became abundantly clear that the salesman had done an excellent job and the buyer was simply prevaricating about signing an order. The lesson here is that a good salesperson should never be frightened of asking for the order. During another field accompaniment with a less experienced salesperson, we

A GOOD SALESPERSON SHOULD NEVER BE FRIGHTENED OF ASKING FOR THE ORDER.

ONE OF THE UNSTATED OBJECTIONS WILL COME FROM THE FACT THAT PEOPLE JUST DON'T LIKE BEING SOLD TO!

were attending the third sales appointment during which the salesperson was, in effect, playing ping pong with the prospect. Having been introduced as someone from the HR department at the beginning I had to intervene because I could see that the buyer wanted the product and I suggested that the salesperson simply handed the order over for signature. The prospect smiled took the order and signed it and we were quickly on our way. The salesperson was furious with me and told me never to intervene in a sales call. I said in response; " *I completely understand I should have let you fail but as you have not hit your target for the last two months my instinct was to help. Please ensure that you do not fail to meet your target this month!*"

There are many reasons why a follow-up call may be required following the initial discovery call. Every effort should be made to seek to close the sale, but a follow-up call may be requested by the prospect. If the salesperson has done an effective job in creating interest, establishing need and overcoming all objections, the only reason for a follow-up call should be that the prospect needs approval to sign an order or that there is a need for others to be involved in the administration of the order. The salesperson should clarify exactly what is the purpose of the next call and should either book this call immediately or gain agreement to a follow-up to secure the date of the next appointment. In many cases, a successful discovery will result in a request for a full quotation. In some cases, this can be done there and then, and the salesperson can move to a close. In more complex product and service sales situations, the quotation may be more complicated at which point the salesperson should ask what will happen when the quotation is received, who will be involved in authorisation and if the prospect is merely a key influencer or champion and when the quotation would be assessed. An appointment should be fixed there and then based on that knowledge. Salespeople must be trained always to close for commitment to the next stage in the sales process at all times. The time to close is during the sales call and never subsequently.

I hope this section has provided a better insight into the sales process and the requirement to ensure that all salespeople are given quality training in the subtleties of this fascinating profession.

SALESPEOPLE MUST BE TRAINED ALWAYS TO CLOSE FOR COMMIT TO THE NEXT STAGE IN THE SALES PROCESS AT ALL TIMES.

[1] *Ed Wal: Solution Selling: The Strongman Process(2016) PG Press*

# 2.6 DEVELOP A COACHING STYLE OF LEADERSHIP

The term 'management' is giving way to the word 'leadership' in today's workplace. This reflects major shifts in the attitude to work and the relationship between the individual within the workplace. Today people are only prepared to work for a company that suits their values. People see themselves more as contractors than employees and this impacts the way they prefer to be managed. The old fashioned 'Command and Control' management style, associated with the days when the UK was a more manufacturing-based economy, has given way to a more co-operative leadership style characterised by coaching.

A coaching style of leadership is one in which two people, working as equals in the relationship, have a conversation about one person, namely the coachee. The important word here is 'equal'. This is very different to a style in which the manager sets out the strengths and weaknesses of the individual but instead, allows the individual to think about their performance and develop insights into how they can develop and improve. The power of this style of leadership is that the individual is likely to be more responsive to changes and improvements which THEY have identified. The manager will use a questioning style to focus the coachee on certain aspects of performance and allow them to think about these areas carefully.

Sales managers have traditionally used factual sales performance data to manage and appraise their sales teams but coaching requires a very different mental approach. In coaching there is no power in the relationship, the power is equally shared.

A coaching style of leadership is ideal for the majority of manager / salesperson interactions but not all, as will be mentioned later.

Let's look at a couple of examples of how a coaching style can work very well.

I worked with the Sales Director of a very high-tech company selling specialist products to global corporations. He had a team of four regional sales managers who covered key accounts around the work. He complained to me that he felt the majority of his time was spent dealing with requests from his team for discounts. I asked him to analyse the amount of time this was taking up and it transpired that most of his daily interactions with his team were related to pricing. I suggested to him that the next time he had such a call that he should ask why the discount was required. He reported back on one such conversation after I had coached him on how to handle these situations...

(Manager) *What's the issue?*

(Salesperson) *I need a 15% discount to be able to get this contract from company X*

(Manager) *Why do you think you need a discount?*

(Salesperson) (Taken aback) *Well this a really competitive situation and the buyer is indicating we are expensive*

(Manager) *If you give a 15% discount to a customer who forms a large part of your target then you set a precedent that means the next negotiation with start at 15%. You are demonstrating to them that you have margin to play with.*

(Salesperson) *Well if I don't give them a discount I don't think we will get the order*

(Manager) *What makes you believe that?*

(Salesperson) *Well I lost a recent order which was down to price*

(Manager) *What else do you think you could offer which was not price based but which would be valued by the customer but cost us very little?*

(Salesperson) (Thinking) *Well, I suppose I could offer a technical conference and a factory tour to show them the specialist testing we use*

(Manager) *Anything else?*

(Salesperson) *I could discount the test samples we have to make to participate in the contract, we'd give them away free in some cases anyway*

(Manager) *Anything else?*

(Salesperson) *I could offer a small discount, maybe 5% in addition to the other things*

(Manager) *Anything else?*

(Salesperson) *No, I can't think of anything else just now*

(Manager) *Why don't you try this approach and see if you can win the deal without offering such a big discount*

By taking this approach with all four of his regional managers, the Sales Director was able to dramatically reduce the time he was spending on these pricing discussions. Additionally, the regional managers felt empowered to negotiate with more currencies in their pockets than they had previously considered. The net result was the manager had more time and fewer interruptions, the sales team improved their negotiation skills and the margin recovery on sales grew significantly over the longer term. They discovered that discounting was a very blunt tool which had implications for the future contracts. This is an example of how taking a coaching style makes a big impact on the sales team.

When I was managing a large sales team at MARS DRINKS I found I was receiving daily, weekly and monthly sales reports from my salespeople. These documents showed details of activity such as prospecting calls made, first appointment call made (Discovery) follow-up appointments made, quotations issued, sales made and lost. They also included their pipeline of prospects. Frankly, this mass of paperwork and data was overwhelming. I decided to scrap the lot! I replaced it with one document which was produced at the end of each four-week sales period.

This report combined all the activity information in the previous reports but added in key ratios, namely prospecting calls to the first appointment and appointments to order.

At the end of each sales period, I would arrange to have one-to-one sessions for an hour with each of my sales team. I would go through their reports with them and ask them questions as follows:

(Me) *Talk to me about your period's performance*

(Them) *What do you mean?*

(Me) *Looking at your total sales, you made 7 sales against your target of 10. Clearly that is an issue. Can you explain why you did not hit your target?*

(Them) *There would follow a string of excuses as to why company X said they would sign this month but didn't etc*

(Me) *Well let's look at your key ratios. What do you learn from them?*

(Them) *Prospecting calls to first appointment were high at 20 to 1*

(Me) *Why do you think this ratio is so high?*

(Them) *I don't know*

(Me) *What reasons could cause this high number?*

(Them) *Not targeting the right person?*

(Me) *Anything else?*

(Them) *Not doing enough preparation before the call to understand more about them?*

(Me) *What else?*

(Them) *Not getting past the gatekeeper*

(Me) *Anything else?*

(Them) *Handling the calls better?*

(Me) *Anything else?*

(Them) *Can't think of anything else*

(Me) *What about... xyz*

(Them) *Oh, yes, I hadn't thought about that that*

(Me) *So what do you plan to do about this next month? Which of these do you think are likely to be the main areas for focus?*

(Them) *I will do a, b and c*

(Me) *How can you practice abc*

(Them) *(Explanation)*

(Me) *Good, so let's look at calls to order. Again you are making 10 calls to obtain the order. What do you think about that?*

(Them) *It's too high*

(Me) *What would be a better target?*

(Them) *4 to 1*

(Me) *OK. What can you do to get from 10 to 4?*

(Them) *I don't know*

(Me) *What could be causing this high key ratio?*

(Them) *Not doing enough need creation?*

(Me) *What else?*

(Them) *Going into presentation mode too early*

(Me) *What else?*

(Them) *Not closing for commitment to the next stage or the next appointment?*

(Me) *What else?*

(Them) *I can't think*

(Me) *What about when you are asked for a quotation?*

(Them) *I will send them one*

(Me) *Could you give it to them there and then?*

(Them) *Sometimes yes, I hadn't thought about that*

(Me) *What about when you produce a quotation: What do you do?*

(Them) *I send it to them*

(Me) *How easy is it to get back to them after you have sent it?*

(Them) *Not easy*

(Me) *So how can you make it easier?*

(Them) *Not sure I understand*

(Me) *Could you say to them: 'If I get the quotation to you by say Wednesday, what will you do with it?' If they say that they will discuss it with their boss, ask them when they will do that and then close for an appointment after that to meet up?
It is always easier to get the appointment BEFORE you sent the quote*

(Them) *That's a great idea*

(Me) *So when we go out to work together we know the things we are going to be working on don't we?*

In this interaction, the salesperson feels that they have appraised themselves and will be far more committed to putting these areas into action.

This is an illustration of utilising a coaching style with salespeople. It makes them feel more empowered and also more committed to improving their skills rather than the sales manager taking a more directive approach and telling them what they need to do.

I mentioned earlier that the manager will not always need to use a coaching style of leadership. This comes when, like the above example, the person has not hit their sales target. The salesperson needs to understand that this is not acceptable and must be put right. This is how the manager could approach this aspect of the meeting:

(Me) *Ok so we have agreed on what you are going to be working on next month to reduce your key ratios. Now we need to discuss the fact that you did not hit your target last month. Why is that?*

(Them) (String of excuses)

(Me) *I hear these excuses all the time. The reality is that missing target is not an option and we need to get this put right straight away. You are outside your probationary period and so the business expects you to meet your target. Do you understand this?*

(Them) *Yes. But I am working really hard*

(Me) *That may be so but you are not paid to be busy, you are paid to hit your target. How are you going to hit the target next month?*

(Them) *I have a good prospect file*

(Me) *Looking at it, these names have been there for several months. Are they really going to deliver the goods? Can you put a hand on your heart and say that you are going to meet the target next month?*

(Them) *Not really*

(Me) *So we need to do something different because I am not accepting another missed target next month. What are you going to do:*

(Them) *Well we have agreed to reduce my key ratios which should make me more effective*

(Me) *Agreed but do you think you need to do more prospecting to put more people into the top of your sales funnel?*

(Them) *Yes, I think so*

(Me) *Anything else?*

(Them) *Not really*

(Me) *What about asking for referrals from people you have sold to before or looking to see if you can sell more to the old customers?*

(Them) *That's a good idea. I will try that*

(Me) *Anything else?*

(Them) *Can't think of anything*

(Me) *There's a trade show coming up. Why not buy a ticket and spend the day where there will be lots of prospects all in the same place. Going with a bundle of business cards might be a good idea*

(Me) *What help can I give you to make sure you will hit your target?*

(Them) *You could come with me on a few follow-up calls where I think I have the best chance of a sale*

(Me) *No problem. What else?*

(Them) *Any sales leads which come in would be very much appreciated*

(Me) *I will certainly do what I can but don't rely on these*

You will see a very different approach in this interaction. Firstly, the manager is very firmly telling the salesperson that failure is not acceptable to ensure total focus is made on RESULTS. The manager brings in the good ideas from the previous coaching session but then grills the salesperson into generating new approaches which will help increase sales. this is a more directive approach geared to ensure the salesperson knows that they need to hit target. The sales manager must be seen a helpful and supportive but inflexible when it comes to hitting sales target. This will ensure the salesperson gives total focus to what is needed to meet the target.

Have you noticed the frequent use of the AWE question? And What Else? This is a powerful way to get people's creative juices going and should be used again and again until the other person runs out of ideas at which point you can make further suggestions.

# 2.7 RUNNING EFFECTIVE SALES MEETINGS

Be very honest with yourself and ask yourself how effective are the sales meetings run in your sales team? The reality is that, if you were to run a poll among your salespeople and ask the question you might be very disappointed by the result. The higher-performance members would say that they found the meeting of no value at all and a waste of good selling time. The rest would say that they enjoy the free time and the chance to catch up with other members of the team. From my observation, I rarely see sales meetings run well. Salespeople should leave their sales meeting feeling empowered, excited and re-invigorated.

This is a big ask for the sales manager who is probably inundated with lots of non-sales jobs dumped on him by the organisation that see sales as the general dogsbody. On top of these non-sales jobs and the 'day job' of running the sales team, many sales managers see preparing for the sales meeting as a challenge and a bit of a bore. The net result is that no one gets any real benefit from the meeting.

## SO HOW SHOULD SALES MEETINGS BE RUN?

- First and foremost, sales meetings should be strictly for the benefit of the sales team, not the manager.

- The meetings should actively involve the sales team. There should be a session where they are encouraged to share experiences. They should talk about new things they tried, the problems they encountered and how they overcame them. New ideas for locating good prospects. These shared experiences bond the team and encourage them to share and help each other not only in the meeting but afterwards. This is an invaluable opportunity for the manager to create team bonding. Selling can be a lonely job and the chance to exchange ideas and experience should not be overlooked.

- The manager should use the meetings to highlight excellent performance and to give recognition and reward for good sales statistics but also to spread the love by rewarding other aspects of the last period's activities like prospecting success. They should not simply reward the high performers but give encouragement throughout the team.

- Sales meetings should be a time for formal learning and outside visitors should be brought in. A good idea is to bring in a professional sales trainer to run a session with the team on some aspects of selling. A good example is closing skills or objection handling. The whole team should be actively involved in these sessions and role-playing should be encouraged. Sales managers must run these sessions in a non-judgemental way and encourage their team to actively participate without fear of them being assessed.

- Individual team members should be asked to run a session on some aspect of selling. This participation again bonds the team and helps develop presentation skills which are good for confidence building and help develop future managers.

- The sales meetings should provide an opportunity to sharpen up the sales story to make sure this is fine tuned and embedded within the team. Again practice through role-play is a good idea and team members should be invited to play different roles requiring modifications of the sales story.

- There should be a session to update the team on new product developments or information about the market. It would be useful to have an open session to discuss the competitors and any information brought from the field about the competitors should be encouraged.

- Most importantly, sales meetings should not be too long. Make them half a day with a lunch of sandwiches and coffee during which some fun awards can be given. Make sure the meetings end on a high.

- Following the team meetings, the manager should conduct individual one-to-one sales reviews and encourage the rest of the team to undertake prospecting activity with a prize for the person who makes the most appointments during the time.

- The one-to-one sessions should follow a coaching style as described in the section on developing a coaching style of leadership. Each salesperson should emerge from their review with a clear sense of purpose and very firm objectives for the next sales period.

- At the end of the day, after all the review meetings have been completed the team should reassemble and the manager should give out the fun prizes for prospecting and then ask each member to stand up and tell the team what they have learned from the day and what new insights they will take away with them. The team could be asked what training areas they would like to be covered in the next sales meeting. The team should be asked what part of the sales meeting they found most valuable and enjoyable.

These one-to-one reviews between the manager and salesperson are extremely important and allow the sales manager to conduct a deep dive into the salesperson's activity and results. It is here that the manager should expect the salesperson to come fully prepared to present an analysis of their key ratios and a comprehensive self-analysis of their performance together with areas for focus in the next sales period. The sales manager should expect to see a comprehensive plan of activity for the forthcoming sales period at which point any deficiencies and gaps should become clear. Whilst the manager should be seen as a strong leader, they must at all times make it very clear that a failure to meet target is not acceptable and salespeople need to understand this very clearly. Sales managers who allow themselves to be bamboozled with excuses are their own worst enemies. Selling is about results full stop. Any salesperson who has not achieved their target needs to be told that their sales need to be back on target during the next month at which point a collective plan should be put in place to achieve this. The manager should ensure that the salesperson is given every assistance to achieve target because losing a member of the team represents a failure for the company, not just the individual. If the salesperson fails to hit their target in the next month, then the sales manager needs to begin a formal process leading to termination under the terms of the employment contract. If the sales manager has provided every assistance to help an individual get back on track and this has not overcome the problem, then there should be no issue about removing them from the team.

This is how to run a sales meeting. They should be fun, learning opportunities with strong team interaction. They should be a valuable occasion for team bonding and shared experiences. The smart sales manager should recognise that sales meetings should be the highlight of the month and not a dreaded time that requires lots of work for them.

Managers increasingly conduct remote monthly reviews using e-mail and Zoom. Too often the sales meetings are a one-way process driven by the sales manager. This is one area of sales management which can be dramatically improved. If correctly conducted the monthly sales meeting should be a driver of sales productivity and really must be given far greater importance. The meetings should provide a focus for sales skills development and learning and most importantly should be a two-way in style.

Wherever possible, sales meetings should take place physically and not virtually. There will, of course, be situations where this is not possible for example when the sales teams are separated geographically but from observation physical meetings generate a positive vibe which cannot be re-created virtually. Selling can be a lonely experience and the opportunity to get together with fellow

colleagues and share experiences should not be underestimated. Sales managers should invest a decent amount of time thinking about and preparing their meetings. The salespeople should play an active role in these meetings.

A results-focus is a vital component of sales team management, and the manager should not shy away from revealing good and bad performance. Everything in a sales team should be transparent. The manager should show the key ratios across the entire sales team so that the ratios of successful salespeople become apparent and can be used as a benchmark for individual assessment. Individuals who have particularly impressive key ratios should be asked to explain what they do to achieve them. Shared experiences are of great value.

Sales managers should consider making every sales meeting a learning experience and inviting external participants is an excellent way to make these meetings memorable. The Mars Group used some amazing external training agencies that were particularly good at making sales training exciting and impactful. I would regularly invite one of the trainers to my monthly team meetings to ask them to run a session on a particular aspect of the sales process and to conduct role-playing exercises as part of the session. At the end of these sessions, the salespeople would be asked for their feedback on the learning experience and the team were asked for suggestions for future training at the next sales

meeting thus making training a collective activity and not one imposed by the manager. Sales training should be an ongoing process carried out by the manager during field accompaniment, and at sales meetings and not restricted to periodic training courses. The sales manager will of course have had access to the monthly sales reports in advance of each meeting and so will be able to report on the team's pipeline and collective forecast for the next month. This will highlight any issues about the team achieving future sales targets and the team should be asked what they could be doing to ensure that the team performance is ahead of target and collective commitment should be sought. The monthly sales meetings should be pacey and action-packed with a high level of momentum. Sales managers should be given training on presentation skills and should be encouraged to ensure that visual information is presented to the highest standard.

So the message from this section is that sales meetings should be seen as a driver of sales productivity. The sales team should look forward to these meetings as an opportunity to share experience, to learn and refine selling skills and have detailed appraisals with their manager.

SELLING IS ABOUT RESULTS FULL STOP.

# 2.8 MAKING THE BEST USE OF THE CRM SYSTEM

From observation, CRM systems can often be one of the biggest causes of sales management taking their eye off the sales ball. It tends to focus attention on activity at the expense of results. I should state that I am not anti-CRM. Used correctly it can be a fantastic asset to any business. However, my experience has been that it can tie up a huge amount of sales management time and may not always have a measurable impact on sales productivity. Let's understand the primary purpose of a CRM system. At its heart, it is a way to organise salespeople in such a manner that all stages in the buying process from suspect through to sale and into customer loyalty are tracked, documented and diarised. The CRM system should ensure that all correspondence relating to a customer and prospect is stored and accessible and that the next contact is scheduled in the diary, never to be forgotten.

A CRM system, when used as an enterprise system will ensure that no two salespeople will be prospecting for the same company at the same time without a full awareness of all historical and current activities and contacts with that company. It will ensure that any pricing and discount structure is clearly identified for all customers. Companies will often go further and ensure that the CRM system tracks every quotation and every order that is transacted with every customer. I have heard many justifications for a CRM system but one that is common is that, should a salesperson or key account manager be run over by a London bus, the system will ensure that someone else can pick up the pieces and run with them since nothing will be held exclusively in someone's head.

What happens, in reality, is that the installation of a CRM system can be enormously disruptive for the company and take the eye off the sales ball. One of the first processes is to load data into the system. This can be a very frustrating process because companies are not always efficient in how they store their data. This can lead to humorous and often embarrassing results. I remember one source of data came in from the telesales function where operators would frequently append data into the database which resulted in mailings to customers with the salutation "Dear Miserable\*\*\*\*\*\*\*"! Data migration which is the posh name for the process of a customer attempting to integrate its data into the CRM database, can be a challenging one and the old adage of *"rubbish in rubbish out"* is highly applicable here.

The next phase in setting up the CRM is to set out the sales process stages that are to be reported upon and this is where the seeds are sown for an unhealthy focus on activity levels. More on this later.

In an ideal world, I can fully appreciate the desirability of having a master computer system which captures and tracks every single contact with a company as well as holding details of all correspondence, quotations and orders over time. The trouble is that we do not live in an ideal world and the convolutions that a business can be put through in an attempt to realise this Nirvana are so often not worth the considerable cost and effort that goes into it. I would say that over my career I have rarely encountered an organisation with a CRM system which clearly and positively impacts sales productivity. This is a shocking statement to make but maybe once again relates to the fact that I am brought into companies who have problems with their sales productivity. The size of the CRM industry would suggest that it must be effective it's just that I haven't seen it!

In one role I had as a consultant I was asked to recommend a suitable CRM system and to manage the implementation across six different companies in the group. Having agreed upon a proposed system and accepted the not inconsiderable budget, the process was bogged down by the lack of availability of managers willing to dedicate time for data integration and meetings required to agree on the reporting systems for all six companies. Different companies had different sales processes that they wished to analyse which made it very difficult to arrive at one common reporting structure. Gaining a compromise solution took a great deal of time.

Possibly the biggest problem came when the system was launched and it was required that all salespeople and sales managers had to use the system. The CRM supplier had undertaken extensive

> **THE PROBLEM IS THAT COMPANIES TRY TO DO TOO MUCH WITH THEIR CRM SYSTEM.**

> **I WOULD SAY THAT OVER MY CAREER I HAVE NEVER ENCOUNTERED AN ORGANISATION WITH A CRM SYSTEM WHICH CLEARLY AND POSITIVELY IMPACTS SALES PRODUCTIVITY.**

training with sales managers and salespeople to familiarise them with the system. However, the use of the system was not mandated by the senior management with the result that very few people actually used it and very quickly people forgot how to use it. The net result was that the introduction of CRM was a disaster. This is an experience I would suggest is not at all uncommon.

The problem is that companies try to do too much with their CRM system. I believe that a phased process is likely to be far more effective and will ensure that all users will buy into it on a progressive basis. There are simple CRM systems available like SET4 which are almost glorified diary management systems for salespeople. I do not regard this as a derogatory description because salespeople who are working hard generate a lot of information and a great deal of follow-up activity. A simple CRM system should provide the primary desktop dashboard for a salesperson connecting contact data, letters, emails, quotations and orders with a diary management system. Used at this level the CRM will become the salesperson's friend ensuring that follow-up calls and meetings are not forgotten and that all correspondence relating to a customer or prospect is available through one desktop function. Achieving this functionality in a CRM system will be considerably easier than aiming for the full functionality described earlier and will gain the sales team's buy-in and confidence far more quickly.

## SALES MANAGERS AS "DESK JOCKEYS"

So assuming that a simple form of CRM as described above is available to the sales manager we come to one of the major problems that I have seen in my work with clients. This is where sales managers become *"CRM Desk Jockeys"*, a wonderfully descriptive term used by Mike Weinberg in his brilliant book *Sales Management. Simplified.*[1] The CRM reports will show the number of contacts made by salespeople at all stages in the buying process. The reports can easily calculate key ratios and can be presented in a very attractive manner. The problem is that managers can become overly focused on activity and less on results. I have said several times in this book that results are the only thing that really matters and that activity levels are to be used to focus training on sales skills. A manager cannot rely totally on CRM reports to manage their sales team which is a real danger when a sexy CRM system, with its colourful charts, provides a tempting alternative to getting out in the field and working with salespeople at the sharp end.

Sales managers need to know what is in the pipeline at any time. Specifically the pipeline at the end of the sales process which represents the bank of sales awaiting conclusion. This is the information that the sales manager will use to provide the company with forecasting and cash flow management. It is therefore a vital measure for the company. Reliance upon the CRM system alone for pipeline information can be very dangerous indeed and I have seen time and again situations where the pipeline forecast bears little relationship to reality. Sales managers who do not spend the right amount of time in the field with their salespeople will be totally reliant upon the judgement of those salespeople whose orders are likely to be closed over the next four weeks. Anyone who has ever managed salespeople will know that the optimism and self-belief of salespeople can often be unreliable.

So the message is very clear. Companies that dump too many non-sales activities on the desk of sales managers run the risk that they spend inadequate amounts of time working in the field with their salespeople to sharpen their skills and increase their sales effectiveness. It is only by working closely with salespeople that the sales managers will be able to use their direct observation to assess pipeline forecasts which are so critical to the management of the company as a whole. Companies should be very cautious about installing a CRM system and make sure that they know exactly what the primary purpose of such a system is to be. My advice would be to start simple, get it working with everyone using it properly before adding further elements to it. Most importantly sales managers must avoid becoming overly focused on the activity reports provided by a CRM system.

ANYONE WHO HAS EVER MANAGED SALESPEOPLE WILL KNOW THAT THE OPTIMISM AND SELF-BELIEF OF SALESPEOPLE CAN OFTEN BE UNRELIABLE.

[1] *Weinberg M, (2016) Sales management. Simplified Published by HarperCollins Leadership.*

# PART THREE:
## NEW BUSINESS AND KEY ACCOUNTS

## CONTENTS

## 3.1 GETTING TO GRIPS WITH NEW BUSINESS: THE ENGINE OF LONGER-TERM GROWTH

Let's, first of all, get it out in the open... there is no secret to success in new business! If you were hoping for some magic bullet sales technique that would transform your new business, I'm sorry but I'm going to have to disappoint you. If I think about the salespeople that I have worked with over the years and put to one side those superstars who just transcend the norm, the common trait that defines successful salespeople is that they just work harder than everyone else! There are many salespeople who are not successful and yet have a high work rate. The difference between them and successful salespeople is that successful people work smarter, they understand the principle of the sales funnel and instinctively know that if they fail to put in prospects at the top of the funnel for any period of time they will suffer later as night follows day. You get out what you put in.

There is absolutely no doubt that good salespeople share common personality traits. They like meeting people and they have naturally good interpersonal skills. They are chameleons and can instinctively assess a prospect's personality and adjust their style and presentation accordingly. Good salespeople are goal orientated and they like to win and generally like to be appreciated as winners. They also try not to fool themselves and make excuses for not delivering.

SUCCESSFUL PEOPLE WORK SMARTER

THE COMMON TRAIT THAT DEFINES SUCCESSFUL SALESPEOPLE IS THAT THEY JUST WORK HARDER THAN EVERYONE ELSE!

New business salespeople have other recognisable traits. They have high energy; they are self-motivated, and they are resilient. This resilience trait is a vital component of the new business salesperson who recognises that selling is a numbers game. Not every telephone call will get through to a prospect. Not every prospect call will result in an appointment. Not every sales call will result in a sale. However, they know that if they undertake enough of these calls and they have belief in their sales skills then the numbers will follow.

## RECRUIT EFFECTIVELY AND CONSTANTLY

For the above reasons, sales managers need to develop highly effective recruitment processes when hiring new business salespeople. We have already looked at this process in great detail in Part Two. Working with the HR department, time spent thinking about ways to identify if candidates possess the personality traits described above will pay huge dividends in terms of saving recruitment costs and getting new recruits successfully through their probationary periods. The Mars group that I worked for in my early career was very well known for its recruitment processes. A pool of potential candidates is whittled down to a final group who are then put through a weekend recruitment programme. Good salespeople are very good at selling themselves and reliance upon a single interview may not be the most effective way to get under the skin of the candidate. The weekend group recruitment process, whilst tying up valuable management time, has proved time and again to be a most effective way of identifying genuine talent. Mars is one of the largest privately owned corporations

**RUNNING YOUR OWN RECRUITMENT WEEKENDS AND FINANCIALLY REWARDING CANDIDATES WILLING TO GO ONTO A WAITING LIST COULD BE A FINANCIALLY ASTUTE DECISION.**

in the world and so this approach to recruitment has clearly proved to be successful. There are many personality-profiling tools that can be used to identify particular personality traits and these can be completed ahead of the weekend programme. When I ran recruitment programmes like this, I would put candidates in pairs and give them selling tasks to achieve like getting through the gatekeeper, going through a discovery process but most of all observing the degree to which individuals listen as opposed to talking. I would also take the role of a prospect and see the extent to which the salesperson would identify if I was a real decision maker with a budget as well as establishing interest in the product leading to the identification of a need. Most importantly I would look for the degree to which the salesperson would close for further commitment when the opportunity arose.

So adopting effective sales recruitment programmes will reduce your salesforce turnover and get new recruits hitting their targets earlier. I have mentioned previously that sales managers should constantly be on the lookout for new sales talent and therefore running periodic recruitment weekends will ensure that they have candidates in the wings when needed. If your company is offering an attractive package, candidates may be willing to go through such a process in order to enter a waiting list. Considering the considerable costs charged by recruitment companies, running your own recruitment weekends and rewarding candidates willing to go onto a waiting list could be a financially astute decision.

153

# GET NEW RECRUITS OFF TO A SOLID START

So having recruited people with the required traits and personalities to work in new business, the sales manager must provide an excellent induction programme, the highlight of which is training in the sales pitch. I have already mentioned the importance of the sales story, but this is a critical part of arming the new business salesperson with the value proposition for your product or service. Salespeople naturally like to talk and can easily move into presentation mode before establishing interest and need. I have seen many sales presentations which focus on the company, its headquarters, its impressive R&D facilities, its huge factory and pictures of its branded lorries and vans. None of this is of interest to a prospect in the process of establishing interest and need. These things can be of value when overcoming objections once we are in the closing stage of the sale.

I mentioned earlier the principle of the sales funnel. This is in reality a model which shows the process of sale from prospect to loyal customer and neatly illustrates the need to put as many prospects as possible into the mouth of the funnel in order to feed a constant flow of qualified prospects into the working day. The visual concept of a pipeline is a great way of understanding that if you stop putting in at one end then the flow will dry out quickly at the other.

## DEVELOP EFFECTIVE PROSPECTING HABITS

Another part of the salesperson's induction should be a clear presentation of the target market and clarification of the ideal customer. Prospecting the wrong target market will result in a high ratio of calls to order and thus reduced sales productivity. So let's take a look at sales prospecting. There is a more detailed section on sales prospecting in Part Two. Many salespeople are frightened and resistant to this process and I fail to understand why. In some, it's the fear of rejection and an inability to recognise that it's just a numbers game. Hopefully, the recruitment process mentioned earlier will ensure you have new business salespeople with the resilience to cope. In the old days prospecting was synonymous with cold-calling which can be a soul-destroying activity. Today we have many powerful tools at our disposal to help us prospect efficiently. I would strongly recommend that sales managers spend some time in prospect training as part of the induction programme.

LinkedIn can be an extremely valuable tool and the Sales Navigator module allows the salesperson to identify prospects which fit the target market quite accurately. This can provide an initial database for further prospecting. Sending 10 In-Mails to this prospect list every day will take no more than 10 minutes, especially

PROSPECTING THE WRONG TARGET MARKET WILL RESULT IN A HIGH RATIO OF CALLS TO ORDER AND THUS REDUCED SALES PRODUCTIVITY.

if the salesperson has already drafted a short and effective introductory message. Undertaken systematically, that's 200 prospecting messages every four-week sales period. A more refined prospecting can be undertaken by spending half an hour every day reading the business sections of newspapers and browsing industry-relevant publications to identify companies and people who look worthy of prospecting. For example, an article featuring a new recruit to a prospect company could be valuable information as new people are more likely to be receptive to consider new sales arguments. LinkedIn can be used to find out more information about these people and enable more relevant and personalised messaging to be sent. Equally, information in the business press and trade publications may highlight companies on the up and once again searching LinkedIn for the relevant decision-makers in those companies will help populate the growing database.

Since COVID, new business prospecting has become complicated by the growing trend of home working. LinkedIn has become even more valuable as a result because most individuals registering for LinkedIn will keep their information up to date and will provide a vehicle for effective communication via their contact information or through the built-in messaging service. This reduces the wastage of prospecting messages.

Salespeople are notoriously frightened of the telephone which in my opinion is one of the most powerful tools at their disposal. I can fully understand why allocating whole chunks of time to prospect calling on the telephone can feel like pulling teeth, but I'm a great believer in the 'little and often'

SINCE COVID, NEW BUSINESS PROSPECTING HAS BECOME COMPLICATED BY THE GROWING TREND OF HOME WORKING.

mantra. Picking five different prospects from your database every day who have already been sent messages via LinkedIn and calling them will result in 100 prospect calls per four-week sales period. As I said, it's a numbers game. Continuing with LinkedIn, a salesperson should ensure that they post a relevant and impactful message at least once a week. LinkedIn also has the benefit of allowing the salesperson to identify special interest groups which can be joined, and these impactful messages can be targeted at them as well as the wider LinkedIn audience.

Smart salespeople will explore ways in which they can address numerous potential prospects at the same time. Joining trade associations and Chambers of Commerce as well as special interest groups on LinkedIn provide an opportunity for salespeople to speak on relevant topics and generate contacts for follow-up.

## LEAD GENERATION

In my Mars vending days, we ran huge lead generation programmes using direct mail to generate sales enquiries which were handed to the salesforce to increase the number of appointments they made. We would typically generate 2/3% response rates for a business-to-business mailing which was very cost-effective. Interestingly this revealed some interesting macho traits amongst the sales force. Analysis of the leads which had been passed to the salesforce quickly revealed a very low conversion rate. I explained to the sales teams that the exercise was clearly ineffective and that we were generating poor quality enquiries and therefore the direct mail programme would be terminated. This led to a huge outcry. It turned out that the sales leads **were** extremely valuable in generating qualified appointments but salespeople felt that selling off the back of a sales lead was in some way demeaning of their sales skills. So they would report that the lead was of no value even if it had actually resulted in a sale. I conducted an exercise to compare the names and addresses of the leads which had been generated to the sales generated over the same period and found a remarkable correlation. I could never understand why salespeople took a course of action which significantly shot themselves in the foot! Presenting the salesforce with the results of my analysis made them realise that they should not look a gift horse in the mouth and from that point onwards the conversion rate of sales leads dramatically improved. An interesting insight into salesforce psychology!

When I was running the new business programme for my direct marketing agency, I was trying to get appointments at a very senior level. These people have always been very heavily screened by switchboards and PA's. The most successful lead generation campaign I ever ran involved shoes! Not just any shoes, but Loake shoes which are very high-end shoes handmade in Northampton, the home of shoemaking. I paid a visit to the Loake factory, and they kindly gave me a guided tour which was fascinating in itself. At the end of the tour, I asked my guide if they ever had any unpaired shoes. This question was greeted with some surprise, but it turned out that they had a storeroom full of unpaired shoes which I purchased for £20 a shoe. It should be borne in mind that a pair of Loake men's shoes would typically retail for over £200. In this time of rampant equality, I am very conscious that at the time I targeted the Chairmen of companies that I wanted to meet. It was easier to select men because Loake shoes for men were typically brogues and Oxfords. Choosing shoes to send to female Chairs would have been far trickier as I know from my wife's vast shoe collection! Anyway, I wrote an introductory letter to some 20 Chairmen explaining the capabilities of my agency and ending with the line *"Now I have one foot through the door perhaps you would be interested in seeing the rest of me."* The response to this small mailing exercise was extraordinary. I believe I ended up with appointments with 10 Chairman and several PA's asked if it were possible to have the second shoe to make a pair! I closed some valuable business from this exercise just illustrating how a bit of creativity can unlock potential.

Amusingly I recall one of my London agency competitors trying a similar exercise which involved mailing a live pigeon with a tag attached to its leg to a number of prospect organisations. The idea was that the prospect would be so knocked out by the creativity of the exercise that they would release the bird containing the details of the prospect on the pre-printed tag and create a valuable pool of new prospects. Unfortunately, the exercise was a massive failure because many of the birds arrived dead which caused great upset to the recipients and had an adverse impact on the agency. As if to rub salt in the wound the campaign was picked up by the press further embarrassing the responsible agency.

In order to put as many prospects into the funnel as possible there may be value in recruiting additional resources to support the salesperson but definitely not to replace their own prospecting. Today there is a cheap and often very high-quality resource available to salespeople called Virtual Assistants or VA's. For as little as £30 or £40 a day, a VA can be hired to send more messages to the database. For a little more cost there will no doubt be VA's who would be willing to telephone follow-up messages to try to secure appointments. Using external agencies to book appointments carries a significant risk to the salesperson. Depending on how the VA or external agency is remunerated, meeting the target of appointments booked will often lead to poorly qualified appointments being made and wasting the time of the salesperson.

In my direct advertising days, I bought a telemarketing agency and trained one of the more senior telesales executives to generate my appointments. It took me nearly a year to train this executive to deliver well-qualified appointments during which time I spent a lot of wasted time travelling the motorway network following up badly qualified appointments.

The time spent training the executive was well invested and telemarketing turned out to be a lucrative source of new business and contributed to the £1 million of new business I generated every year for 15 years.

# 3.2 PROSPECTING FOR NEW BUSINESS

Whenever the word prospecting is used it has traditionally raised fear and concern amongst salespeople. The word has historically being associated with cold calling which brings to mind old-fashioned door-to-door salesmanship and timeshare selling which certainly damaged the reputation and prestige of the new business process. Prospecting remains the only way to populate the top of the sales funnel and so It cannot be ignored.

Prospecting in the business-to-business world has certainly changed considerably since the days of the pandemic. Prior to the pandemic prospects tended to be office based or certainly located in their offices permanently. Therefore it was possible to use the telephone and mail system to reach prospects albeit via the dreaded gatekeepers. Post-COVID the world of work has changed dramatically and hybrid working situations are now commonplace and likely to remain so for the foreseeable future. Individuals have found that hybrid working where they work two or three days in the office each week dramatically improves their work-life balance and companies have been forced to accept hybrid working.

Organisations have also benefited from hybrid working because they have been able to scale back on office space and move to hot desking and have come to accept hybrid working as the norm. I believe that hybrid working is now the *"new normal"* and salespeople have had to make significant adjustments to their prospecting strategies.

Prior to the explosion in the use of e-mail, it was possible to run large direct mail campaigns to generate sales leads and enquiries to support a salesforce. Indeed during my time working at Mars Drinks, I ran a very large and systematic direct mail programme which typically generated a 2 to 3% response rate and generated enough leads to support a national sales force. Direct mail has largely been replaced by e-mail marketing and I suspect that the response rates and cost per lead will be dramatically different from the old direct mail days. People are inundated with unsolicited e-mail and have become adept at using junk mail folders to reduce unsolicited mail.

All of this means that the prospecting strategy will require re-thinking. Telephone cold calling can be a soulless activity for anyone, even new business specialists who can cope with rejection. In addition to doing battle with the growing array of gatekeepers (receptionists, personal assistants and executive assistants), hybrid working means that the target may not even be in the office. There has to be another way.

I would suggest that the most efficient prospecting strategy for today's business-to-business market is to have a dedicated and office-based prospecting function within the sales force. It is vital that a comprehensive and accurate database is constructed on the basis that every company within the database meets the desired profile of the organisation in terms of size, sector and contacts. I am of course describing a customer relationship marketing database. The database must ensure that each sales territory has sufficient prospect data to support the territory salesperson. The database can be compiled from many sources and there are many data supply companies in the marketplace that specialise in this. The CRM database needs to have the e-mail addresses of prospects and again any quality data supplier will be able to provide these.

Salespeople are notoriously bad at writing marketing materials and so the office-based prospecting function must include individuals who are competent copywriters and who are well-versed in articulating the sales story for the products being marketed. Salespeople should be discouraged from sending marketing messages themselves.

It is at this point that I have some hard-earned advice with regard to marketing content. Typically marketing messages are all about the company and its wonderful products and how these products can answer the prospect's problems. The reality is that prospects are only interested in one thing and that is having an easy life. Prospects will respond to messages which speak to them and their problems, challenges and issues directly. If messages achieve this then prospects will contact the company far more readily or be amenable to follow-up messages. The e-marketing function should be sending out relevant e-marketing campaigns on a continuous basis ensuring that the salespeople receive copies of all messages which are being sent. The sales team themselves can use their territory databases to telephone prospects knowing that e-marketing messages have been sent to warm up prospects. Telephone prospecting will not only generate appointments but additional data to add to the CRM database. Salespeople should be encouraged to undertake an element of market research everyday reading or scanning trade journals and business pages of newspapers to identify information which could influence their prospecting. For example, many trade publications published details of promotions and recruitments in target companies and this information can be augmented through databases like LinkedIn to provide valuable insights into potential target prospects. In-house marketing functions should make sure that messaging is sent on a regular basis to LinkedIn.

In this way, e-marketing becomes an integrated process with core messaging sent out regularly from the centre and followed up on the telephone by territory salespeople who also add valuable researched information to the database. Sales managers should train salespeople in these research methodologies and monitor activity through sales reporting. One hour spent every day on research can be time very well invested in identifying hot prospects likely to be receptive to sales messages. Similarly, managers should expect salespeople to undertake at least one hour a day on telephone prospecting to build their pipelines. Salespeople are notoriously bad at undertaking these activities and so these should be mandated as part of the sales reporting process and training given by the managers to make sure this work is carried out effectively.

The fact that direct mail Is far less used as a prospecting medium also presents an opportunity for the modern prospecting team. Business people receive much less direct mail today than they did 10 years ago and so well targeted and well designed and copy written direct mail is likely to generate a higher response than it did historically and this is where an accurate and up-to-date CRM system can be very beneficial in ensuring that the targeting information is accurate and up to date. Once again direct mail programmes should not be undertaken by salespeople but by the central marketing function to ensure that materials are well constructed, well designed and on message.

E-marketing programmes can be generated at the territory level to enable sales managers and salespeople to conduct online meetings or webinars which enable them to address multiple prospects with quality presentation materials and these can be a valuable source of new business appointments.

It is a well-known fact that referrals are the very best source of new business and yet I have found that so many salespeople are unwilling to seek them. Every prospecting call should present an opportunity to seek a referral either within the prospect company or outside it.

When speaking to a prospect on the telephone the salesperson should establish if the individual would be involved either directly or as an influencer in the purchase of the products

or services being marketed. If the individual passes this test the astute salesperson should gather information on the entire decision-making group if at all possible and add this to the database. If the individual is not involved or an influencer then the salesperson should be able to obtain details of those people within the organisation who are involved, capture that information and ask to be transferred to the appropriate person. When a sale has been made this is an ideal time to ask for a referral and many salespeople fail to recognise this opportunity.

Clearly, there are other sources of prospects which sales-people can take advantage of. Good examples are trade shows where a £10 entrance ticket can provide a salesperson with a full day of prospect research into a particular market sector. Trade conferences also provide a happy hunting ground for salespeople willing to work the floor.

So the above provides a framework for business-to-business prospecting but considerable benefit can be gained by developing the telephone skills of salespeople. Sales managers should run training programmes using role play to train salespeople in getting through gatekeepers as well as having effective conversations with prospects on the telephone. I have done a lot of training for salespeople to sharpen their prospecting skills on the telephone and training them in objection handling and closing for commitment. Such training pays huge dividends in terms of prospecting effectiveness and builds confidence in the salespeople that will encourage them to prospect on a regular basis.

## 3.3 DECISION-MAKING IN ORGANISATIONS

This book is primarily geared toward organisations selling in a business-to-business environment. In the vast majority of situations where high-value product and service sales are taking place the actual decision-making process can be quite complicated. The concept of MAN (Money Authority and Need) whilst useful in guiding the qualification process, is a slightly simplistic concept. The discovery phase in any sales process needs to establish the exact decision-making process for the product or service in question and to gain an understanding of exactly what role the prospect will play in that purchase process. Let me give you an example. The decision to purchase a new IT system could be quite complex. If we take the example of a Sales Director wishing to buy a CRM system, the decision to purchase may well involve a number of stakeholders. The Sales Director as the internal champion, the IT department, the finance department and, dependent upon the total value of the purchase, it may involve a Board decision. A simple decision to purchase a new photocopier may well involve the premises manager and the finance department about any leasing involvement in addition to the person championing the requirement in the first place.

One of the most complex decision-making processes I ever came across was once again during my time in the Mars group. The KLIX in-cup beverage system developed a hot drink trolley system for use in hospitals. The hospital trolley product was perfectly designed for hospital use. It reduced the time taken by staff in preparing drinks, the avoidance of wasted ingredients and, as the system used disposable plastic cups, it reduced the need for china cups and saucers and the resulting dishwashing process. When all of these factors were taken into account any decision to purchase the hospital trolley system should have been a no-brainer. However, it was the Catering Department that held the budget for ingredient supply. It was a separate department that held the budget for any equipment like the trolley. A separate department held the budget for the china cups and saucers and yet another department was involved in dishwashing. The HR department was responsible for the person pushing the trolley and making the drinks. Another issue was that the hospital; already owned the china and the dishwashing machinery and so the timing of savings due to replacement was extended. The complexity of the decision-making meant that this ideal solution would typically take over a year to get approved.

It is for this reason that business-to-business selling frequently involves several sales meetings and places great importance on the discovery phase of selling by identifying the likely decision-making procedure in the organisation. The experienced salesperson will ensure that their prospect is provided with all the information required to progress a sale internally when the knowledge of the salesperson would not be available. Wherever possible the salesperson should try to create an opportunity to present to all those involved in the decision since only they have the skills and information to overcome any objections which may arise.

## 3.4 KEY ACCOUNT MANAGEMENT: THE DRIVER OF SHORT-TERM GROWTH.

Addressing all the areas we have covered so far in this book will definitely increase your sales productivity. But there is little point in bringing in more new business if you can't retain your existing business, especially the large customers. The Pareto principle states that 80% of your revenue and profit often comes from only 20% of your customers. Even though the actual numbers may not be precise the principle is true in so many cases. If you want to manage a business whose revenue is growing in real terms year on year then retaining your main customers, otherwise known as your key accounts, is a priority. In any business, there will be a natural churn of existing customers for many reasons. For example, a project may be completed satisfactorily and there is no further work for that customer. A key contact in the customer organisation may leave and their replacement could bring in a favoured competitor. Sometimes organisations put suppliers through a regular review process against your competitors. A customer may well be taken over by a larger company and will be obliged to use incumbent suppliers. There are many natural causes of churn. So the last thing you as a manager need to do is to lose valuable customers through poor intelligence and poor account management.

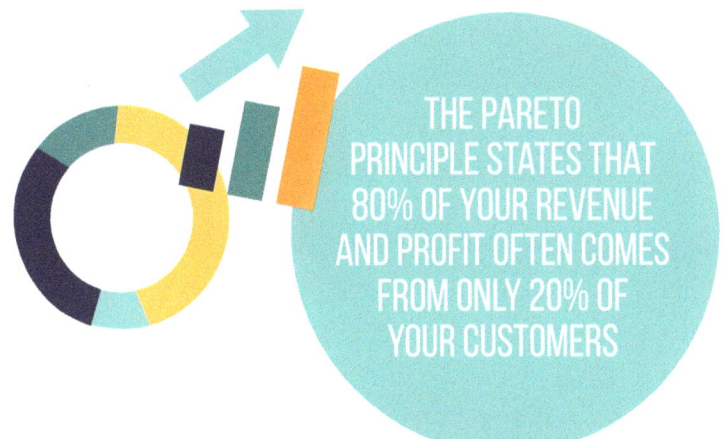

THE PARETO PRINCIPLE STATES THAT 80% OF YOUR REVENUE AND PROFIT OFTEN COMES FROM ONLY 20% OF YOUR CUSTOMERS

Clearly to achieve year-on-year revenue growth your new business activity will need to replace lost business as well. Therefore it's best not to increase this burden by the poor management of your existing customer base.

So what are the mistakes that companies make when it comes to managing existing customers?

- They combine the new business and customer management roles which is rarely an efficient approach for reasons we have already considered

- There is a tendency to take customers for granted and take the eye off the management ball

- Sales managers fail to create account plans for each customer as a basis for efficient account management and review

- Failure to segment customers by size value and potential and allocate the top customers to the best Key Account managers

- The inability to undertake adequate research into the customer to identify alternative buying points

- The inability to ensure that all customer-facing functions are joined up in terms of communications.

These are common themes that I find in my consultancy work. So let us look at how the sales manager should approach the management of existing customers.

1 Of course, companies vary considerably in the number and value of their customers. Some companies operate on single transactions only, but most companies will wish to establish an ongoing relationship with previous customers. Also, the average customer lifetime value will vary considerably from one company to another. In this section, we are really looking at business-to-business companies wishing to retain existing customers.

2 Firstly customers need to be segmented by size and potential. Not all companies have the same potential, and it is a waste of talent to apply great effort in expanding an account if the potential does not exist. This process can be carried out quite easily by internal research and topping up with external discovery.

**③** Customers who have little potential for growth should be managed by more junior account managers whose role is to ensure that customers are receiving a high quality of service in every area in which the company is in contact with the customer. The account manager must be totally responsible for receiving orders and ensuring that they are delivered on time and on budget. They should be the point of contact for the customer and for the delivery departments. I have come across many situations in which the account manager is blissfully unaware of a late delivery, or a poor installation simply because the internal systems are not adequate. There is of course an element of company culture here that we considered earlier in the book. If the company culture is universally pro-sales, then the dangers of miscommunication will be significantly reduced. The account manager needs clear and simple systems to maintain total visibility of all orders going through the system for each of the customers under their management.

**4** Account managers should conduct periodic reviews with each customer under their management. Ideally, this should be done every six months but certainly no less than once a year. If possible, account reviews should be carried out face to face but where this is not possible by Zoom or a similar audio-visual method. The review should be standardised and structured to ensure the following areas are covered:

a Is the customer generally happy with the service being provided?

b Are there any areas where the company can improve?

c Explore if there are any ongoing or future changes within the customer organisation which could affect the company

d To thank the customer for their business.

e Sometimes, if the relationship is warm the customer may reveal information which is "off the record" which could be of value to the company like a change in organisational structure or a change in personnel.

**5** Commission plans for account managers should obviously be based on turnover on a year-on-year basis. This provides a quantitative basis for remuneration. A useful qualitative element for review purposes can be gained through the use of an annual customer survey which we have mentioned previously. These surveys can be carried out by external companies and provide extremely valuable feedback to the organisation as a whole

So the management of small but repeat purchasing customers should be relatively straightforward and will enable the company to develop the skills of account managers over time. As account managers become more and more skilled and proficient, they can be given larger key accounts to manage as they develop their career paths. Let's now look at those extremely important customers who frequently represent as much as 80% of the business. Clearly, these customers need to be managed by account management staff who are trained and experienced. These are your key account managers.

So how do you define a key account? The answer to this question may not be as obvious as you think. David Ventura and Phil Jesson in their excellent book on key account management, *Top 10 Tips for Your Top 10 Customers*[1] offer the following potential definitions for a key account:

- Are they your largest customers by volume looking back in time?

- But should history come into it? It may be perfectly reasonable to consider a key account to be not only a major customer but also a major prospect with the greatest potential value.

- Are there key accounts which are coming up for major contract renegotiation?

- They could be major customers that have had some serious issues with your products and service and are now in *"intensive care"*.

- Perhaps key accounts are those where you are making an 'unacceptable' profit and so you need to justify this by delivering an exceptional level of service.

- Key accounts might also be important lost customers that you want to win back.

- Or they could be a dream prospect that you would like in the future, the kind of organisation that would change the fortunes of your business if you had them on board.

- They could be a competitor's major customers that are vulnerable for a period of time. For example, if a competitor's key account manager has recently moved on, their vacant territory might present a window of opportunity for a short period of time.

- And whilst on the subject of competitors, a key account might be one of your major customers that is being targeted and courted by your competitors. Do you know who these accounts are?

- Key accounts could also be a customer where if you lost them your business would feel the repercussions immediately with major consequences like redundancies or cutbacks. if you have a multi-site customer operation with dozens of people across the country you might simply ask your managers to work on three accounts that are vital to their branch and then allow the team to tell you what their criteria are for a key account.

- You should allow your Finance Director to have a say. For them perhaps the key accounts are the 20% of customers generating 80% of the profits. They would say that profit is the thing that matters.

- And what about those small accounts that spent next to nothing but have huge prestige value, the sort of door-opening names that when you mention them in the marketplace, prospects say "Wow! If you are working with them then maybe, you had better come and talk to us"

Ventura and Jesson are acknowledged experts in the whole area of key account management and the list above illustrates that key account definition may not be that straightforward. I have recommended their superb book to many clients, and I also use several of their key account management tools in my work. It would make good sense for your sales management team to spend some time gaining clear agreement as to the definition of a key account which your company feels most comfortable with and this process should certainly consider the list above.

Ventura and Jesson place great importance on developing a partnership relationship with a key account. What do they mean by a partnership relationship? By this, they mean that the relationship between company and customer transcends the purely transactional or supplier status. A customer with whom you have a partnership relationship will have a number of key attributes:

- They will be willing to have formal key account review sessions maybe as frequently as every three months.

- They will be willing to share detailed information about their company and the company's future plans. They may even divulge confidential information which could be of great value to you.

- A partnership relationship will have multi-level relationships. I see so many key account relationships based on single contacts at the customer level. This is potentially dangerous.

- The customer will generally accept your recommendations on products and services.

- They will see your company as a source of innovation and fresh thinking. In other words, they see you as 'adding value' to the relationship.

- There is little resistance to price and price increases.

- They will be willing to give you referrals and testimonials.

- Very importantly, they will be reasonable and constructive when there are problems.

Ventura and Jesson have come up with 20 partnership indicators, but I would strongly recommend that in the key account strategy review that you carry out in your own organisation, you identify your own list which suits your company and its relationship with its customers and which can be used to define the kind of key account relationship and partnership that you wish. You should aim for at least 10 such indicators.

Each key account manager should be required to put a tick or a cross against each of these indicators for every one of the accounts under their management. This should be used in the key account plan which should be constructed for every key account. What should the key account plan look like...?

179

- First of all, it should have all the corporate information relating to the customer including the ownership, location of the head office and any subsidiaries.

- The trading history in terms of profit and revenues clearly showing the graphical history. Again, a moving annual total will clearly illustrate the trends over the previous twelve months.

- A management structure as it relates to the buying function and clear identification of key buying personnel and their authority. Several organisations that I have worked with have included notes which illustrate where relationships with the company are strong, average or weak.

- The plan should have clear targets in terms of financial performance and importantly progress with regard to the partnership indicators. For example, if a 10-point partnership indicator is in place and a particular key account has a tick in say 5 boxes, then the key account manager should identify how they will be increasing this to say 7 ticks over the course of the review period.

- An alternative approach to key partnership indicators is to rank each on a scale of 1 to 5 or 1 to 10. This will enable a more detailed and precise assessment of the partnership relationship.

[1] *Ventura D & Jesson P (2019) Top 10 Tips For Your Top 10 Customers New Generation.*

**MASTERING SALES LEADERSHIP**

- The development potential should be clearly identified, and clear targets and action plans written down. A good example of this is where the customer is clearly divisionalised along activity, product or brand basis and where the company is not yet trading with all divisions. The plan could be to open up access to another trading division and to have gained the first order within the review period. This should be followed up with specific action plans which could include asking existing customer contacts to provide a referral to other divisions and to have undertaken a presentation to another division and secured opportunities to quote.

If customers are managed in the way outlined above the company will have the greatest opportunity to retain its existing business and maximise the opportunities to grow and develop those accounts that it deems to be key accounts. Segmenting customers into accounts and key accounts will provide the appropriate level of focus for individual account managers. It will ensure that the most experienced people are looking after the most valuable accounts. It will also provide a clear development pathway for account management people within the organisation.

We have therefore addressed the way sales managers need to clearly separate new business from existing business management. This, on its own, will increase sales productivity by ensuring that the right people are in the right jobs. Natural hunters are targeted at new business and natural nurturers are targeted at existing customers. Furthermore the existence of detailed plans for both new business and existing business provide a clear focus for review against results, not simply activity.

# PART FOUR:
## GETTING IMPROVEMENTS IN SALES PRODUCTIVITY IN 90 DAYS

# GETTING IMPROVEMENTS IN SALES PRODUCTIVITY IN 90 DAYS

So, having got to this stage in the book, you might be thinking that there is an awful lot to do. You might be wondering where to start. That's quite normal. The purpose of this section in the book is to suggest how you can approach the first 3 months in order to see rapid results.

## CORPORATE CULTURE

Sales Directors can do much to improve the company culture and ensure that the business is 100% pro-sales:

- At the next Board Meeting, the Sales Director should raise this with the Board and gain agreement to conduct an employee survey to identify areas for improvement. The Sales Director should ideally have a few anecdotes to plant the thought that maybe there are departments within the business which are negative about the sales function. An employee survey is not expensive and can be carried out quite quickly, certainly giving results within 8 weeks.

- The survey should be constructed in such a way as to highlight attitudes towards the sales function and should be extended to include the sales team.

- Armed with the results, the Sales Director should get the external survey company to present the results to the board to avoid any feelings that they have an axe to grind.

- The Board should then debate the findings and identify key areas for improvement. If the findings are serious then the Managing Director should take responsibility for the process and ensure that the implementation programme is fully committed to and reported upon at every board meeting. Delegating upwards is a great idea here as the Managing Director is the only person who can create the mandates to address areas for improvement.

## PLANNING

It's probably too late to change the current plan for this year. However, now is the time to allocate time in your diary to start preparing for next year's planning cycle. In many organisations, the planning cycle starts earlier and earlier so here's what you can do to ensure that next year's plan is realistic and achievable...

- Look carefully at the last two or three years' sales. Calculate how much business from one year repeats in the next. This will give you a feel for churn. Customers will not repeat the previous year's sales for a number of reasons. They may have given you a project which was completed and so there was no more to do. Or they could have moved to a competitor. Either way, you need to know. Doing this over 3 years if at all possible, will give you a very good indication of annual churn rates. There are two things to do with this information:
  - Allocate a churn figure against the coming plan to ensure it is factored into the existing customer business targets.

- Make sure that you are able to identify why a customer is not trading with you and flag this to the relevant account manager. Too often a drop in sales from one customer is not picked up quickly enough and new trading relationships, once established, are very difficult to retrieve. This is a function of the existing and key account management teams.

• Calculate sales productivity in both the new business team and the account management team. Do this on a Moving Annual Total basis (MAT). From this calculate the average productivity per salesperson. The MAT analysis will tell you if sales productivity is on the rise or declining. Ensure you set up systems to calculate sales productivity every month to create new MAT figures which will identify trend data highlighting sales productivity in both new business and existing account areas. This will demonstrate the effectiveness of the actions you are taking based on implementing the ideas within this book.

- Work with your Marketing Director to create a market overview, looking at the key trends within your market sector which are likely to impact sales in the coming year. Also, conduct a competitor analysis to identify areas for focus in terms of pricing and new product development.

- It would be useful to construct a SWOT analysis of your company and compare it with your major competitors. This will identify areas for change.

- Construct a product lifecycle analysis to see how your products line up as cash cows, dogs, superstars and decliners. This will identify key areas for new product development.

## MANAGEMENT WORKING PRACTICES
### Conduct detailed review sessions with each sales manager

- Speak to each of your sales managers and ask them what their task load is and identify areas which do not relate to their key function of generating sales revenues. Make sure these ancillary tasks are reassigned elsewhere.

- Then ask each manager to identify the amount of time they are spending in the field working with their salespeople. You should include this in your monthly reporting system with your sales managers. You should expect to see that they are spending at least one day every month with each of their salespeople.

- Look at the roles of salespeople within each team and see if any salespeople are given new business and account management targets. If they are, give VERY serious consideration to getting them to focus on their key areas of strength and not mix roles.

- Look in detail at both new business and account management functions within the whole sales team. Look at productivity data for both and agree with sales managers if right people are in the right roles. This will highlight recruitment priorities.

- Review the recruitment processes being taken for both new business and account management roles and consider changing them to the approach suggested in this book.

- Analyse existing accounts and satisfy yourself that they are being classified by potential (Tier 1/2/3 etc) and allocated to the most appropriate account manager.

- Review the sales reporting systems in use and encourage sales managers to reduce paperwork to the documents they really need to run monthly review session. Do encourage them to have key ratio sections.

- Get all sales managers to read the section on running sales meetings and then have a discussion with each manager about what they have taken out of this section and how they plan to change their way of working.

- Consider hiring a sales coach to train all your managers (and yourself) on how to coach and specifically how to coach within your specific business. Conduct monthly reviews with the coach and the managers to ensure that progress towards a coaching style of leadership is being created.

- Training: The Sales Director should ask the training department or external sales training company what training programmes are in the pipeline and to assess the importance and impact they are having. It may be a great idea to have the training agency present a review so that the Sales Director can get a feel for the work being done and if there would be merit in looking at alternatives. Other training organisations should be asked to conduct a review before pitching for their proposed programmes. Getting the incumbent to pitch alongside will be educational.

- Voice of the Customer Survey: Bearing in mind that the driver of the current year's growth will come from existing customers, it is very worthwhile carrying out a 'Voice of the Customer' survey. This can be done by an external agency and the feedback will highlight just how well existing customers are being managed, how valuable they see the relationship with your company and highlight areas for improvement. This data should form part of the input to the new plan and guide the sales managers in managing the existing account team.

## Conduct a review of the CRM system

- Assess the quality of data being held.

- How much do salespeople use it? Is it seen as an essential tool? If not understand why not. Task all managers to mandate that working with the CRM is not optional. It needs to become the desktop system used by all salespeople and should incorporate email, quotation systems, diary management and word electronic notetaking. There is only one way to use CRM and that is to make it fully embedded into the daily working methods of everyone. Without a mandate, it will not happen. Delegate this mandate to each sales manager but do ensure you keep a close eye on implementation.

- Identify the way CRM data can create monthly reports, pipeline reports, key ratios etc.

It looks like a lot, but in practice, the astute Sales Director should be able to delegate much of the work both upwards and downwards. In conducting such an approach, the new sales productivity data being generated will clearly demonstrate the impact of the changes and calculate the actual return on investment from carrying out this work.

# PART FIVE:
# HOW WILL EMERGING TECHNOLOGY IMPACT SALES LEADERSHIP OVER THE NEXT FIVE YEARS?

194

# HOW WILL EMERGING TECHNOLOGY IMPACT SALES LEADERSHIP OVER THE NEXT FIVE YEARS?

Artificial Intelligence (AI) is already predicted to make huge changes in our lives. As I write ChatGPT has already achieved 100 million active users within two months of its launch. The pessimists predict it will lead to the end of humanity, but, ever the optimist, I would like to think that we will be able to apply some of the huge potential of this amazing developing technology to the development of sales leadership. Managing a sales team can be challenging, especially when dealing with the nuances of the differing personalities, selling styles and customer types. Fortunately, the advances in AI technology will soon begin to transform the way sales managers approach leadership and coaching.

## SALES PLANNING

We have already considered how the development of sales plans based purely upon extrapolation on the previous year's growth data or in line with shareholder requirements can result in plans which are unlikely ever to be hit. This condemns the Sales Director to be on the back foot in the Board meeting. It is always better to produce plans which can be achieved but which are based on careful analysis and also provide scope to be beaten.

AI will provide sales planners with vastly more data analytical capability than ever and open up sophisticated planning tools to smaller companies, not just those with the resources to employ analysts. Algorithms will enable current market data to be combined with historical sales data as well as wider data sources to provide more accurate predictions and market trends as well as identify opportunities and threats which can impact sales.

Customer segmentation will also be made considerably easier with AI tools and algorithms enabling companies to segment their customers based on demographics, industry type and other factors.

Competitor analysis has always been a challenging area in planning. Developing SWOT (Strengths, Weaknesses, Opportunities and Threats) analyses of competitors will be a great deal less biased and more factual if undertaken by machine than man! Access to the huge amount of information on the Internet will provide greater inputs to the competitive environment. Our natural optimism will always seek to put our own products or services in the best light, but AI will do this unemotionally and provide better and more objective insights.

In the 1980's and 90's I ran a very successful direct marketing agency specialising in the Business-to-Business market. One of our USPs was our ability to develop sales support strategies based on the recruitment of customers which would provide the greatest long-term profitability to the client organisation. This would incorporate concepts like Customer Lifetime Value but our approach was a great deal more scientific and went very much further. Client organisations hold a great deal of data about each of their customers. To this, we bought in additional data from organisations like Experian to boost the available client data sets. We then used multiple regression analysis on these data sets. This is a process in which each data point, say age, is compared against another say, colour or location in order to identify which particular characteristic seemed to have the greatest impact upon long-term profitability.

The process was hugely laborious and our Strategist, David Henderson used to rent computer downtime from large organisations to run these analyses. The outcome of this analysis was very profound and resulted in some major marketing and sales insights for large companies. One example was the ability to advise a certain motoring organisation that the characteristic driving profitability was the age of the car not the make and model that it had historically used. This may now seem obvious but our data model was shown to be incredibly accurate when run against the client's actual trading history. For this reason, most new cars began to be sold with very low-cost motor recovery packages and this is now commonplace. The above technique was applied to a wide range of large organisations which had very extensive customer bases (typically banks, building societies, insurance companies and mobile telephone companies).

AI will make such analysis a great deal simpler and quicker and would enable companies to target customer types likely to have greater customer lifetime value than others.

Sales Analytics: AI-driven sales analytics tools will be able to provide real-time insights into the performance of the sales team, including personalised metrics. Such information will help to guide the sales manager by identifying requirements for sales coaching, training and remediation as well as making data-driven decisions about sales team structures and resource allocation.

Sales territory planning has always been a really difficult area for planning. Creating sales territories which balance prospects and existing customers fairly has always been very challenging. AI will make such an analysis easily and enable the Sales Director to identify exactly how many new business sales territories are required to meet sales targets and to map the resulting territories fairly by sales potential.

## AI AND SALES COACHING:

Now this is a very sensitive area for me who earns a living from coaching both sales managers and salespeople! Most coaches believe that computers can never replace experience, natural human empathy and subtlety. However, ChatGPT has demonstrated a remarkable ability to come up with powerful and effective coaching questioning. Additionally, a good coach needs to be able to read nonverbal cues when coaching and be highly responsive to eye movements, skin tone, muscular movements and so on during a coaching interaction.

However, it is becoming very clear that a computer is able to handle both the questioning and interpretation as well as analysing non-verbal cues. However, I believe the human factor will be paramount in the interaction between a coach or sales leader and their team for the foreseeable future.

One essential element is TRUST. In the coaching 'contract' there will be an agreement on confidentiality which is critical to the process. Coaching will not work without the trust that underpins this and I find it difficult to believe that a human will ever give such a high level of trust to a machine. Furthermore, I am reluctant to believe that a machine will be able to fully replicate the one-to-one, human-to-human interaction which is so subtle and nuanced.

Having set out this belief, I can fully accept that AI will (and very soon) provide some incredibly valuable tools to support the leadership coaching process and run alongside it.

There is already an AI tool called Crystal which looks at social media and predicts the personality of potential prospects. This means that for business tools like LinkedIn a pool of prospects can be generated where the individual's personality and communication preferences can be inferred before any contact is made.

This is done by looking at the written style of posts and profiles of individuals in the database and determining where they fit on the DISC range. This makes telephone and email prospecting potentially more effective by pitching communications in ways likely to be more responsive.

Crystal uses a framework called DISC to classify personalities into a few categories that they refer to as D (dominant), I (imaginative), S (stabilizing), and C (conscientious). Every prospect has a primary DISC type in one of these categories and sometimes a secondary DISC type in another.

To keep things simple, Crystal separates these categories into easy-to-remember labels called Archetypes. These are shown on the Personality Map below:

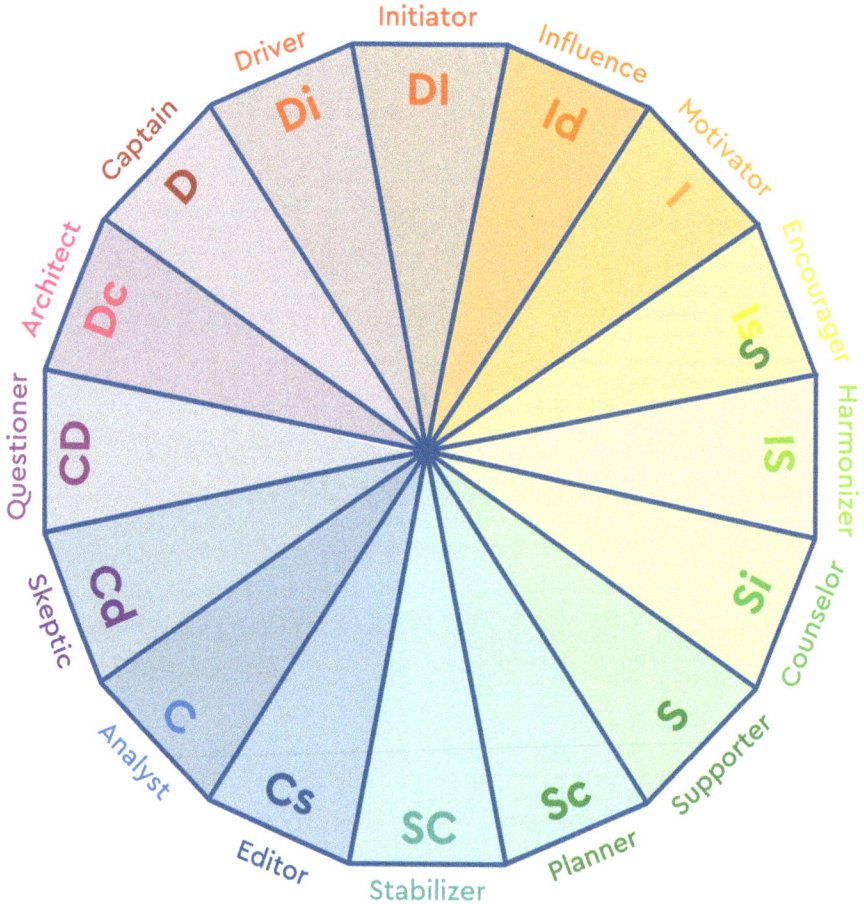

Credit: Crystal website information

Each of the DISC categories is used to define a typology of an individual which will suggest the most effective way to communicate with them to the greatest effect.

Below is a breadown of common personality traits within each of the categories in DISC.

## D personality types
*Captains, drivers, initiators, architects*

- Motivated by control over the future and personal authority
- Tend to prefer instant concrete results and having an advantage over competition
- Communicate clearly and succinctly

## I personality types
*Influencer, motivator, encourager, harmonizer*

- Motivated by innovative, unique, creative ideas and excited by the future
- Tend to prefer building new relationships and experiences.
- Communicate in a casual, expressive way

## S personality types
*Counsellor, supporter, planner, stabilizer*

- Motivated by peace, safety, and others' wellbeing
- Tend to prefer security, reliability and trust
- Communicate in a friendly and genuine way

## C personality types

*Editor, Analyst, Sceptic, Questioner*

- Motivated by logic, information and problem solving

- Tend to prefer accurate information and quality solutions (quality over quantity)

- Communicate in a business-like, fact based way

*Credit: Crystal website information*

Crystal goes further and has created a written style structure for email based upon DISC personality types.

## Email styles for each personality type

Because each of the four DISC personality types tends to communicate differently, there are some key aspects to follow and avoid when emailing.

When emailing more dominant D-types, you should have a clear, conscise subject and body. D-types prefer more formal, but brief emails in which they are called to an immediate action. Be careful not to include a surplus of detail or open-ended questions.

I-types are enthusiastic and energetic, preferring interesting visual aids over lengthy, information blurbs. When emailing I-types, maintain an enthusiastic, casual, optimistic tone. Avoid being too serious or focusing on facts and figures.

 **S-types** love to build personal connections: do this by discussing shared interests. It's important not to skip pleasantries with **S-types**. Be consistent in using a kind, encouraging tone and try not to be forceful or overly direct.

 **C-types** dislike unnecessary pleasantries; they value specific, concrete information instead. Take the time to understand their reasoning for decisions by asking them questions, but do not skip over important information or involve emotion.

*Credit: Crystal website information*

Crystal is a recently launched product and it illustrates how new tools will become available to salespeople to assist them with the challenging task of prospecting which proves time and again to be so difficult for people. Imagine being able to construct an email using absolutely the right communication style to get the prospect's attention. Bearing in mind that prospecting is a numbers game, then moving from a response rate of 2% to 3% will make a very significant difference to the prospect bank for a salesperson. Knowing in advance of a telephone call the best approach to take may increase the hit rate from 1 in 10 to 1 in 5 and therefore doubling the prospecting success.

So, having used AI tools like Crystal to understand the personality type of a Suspect before calling them, AI will, in future, be able to analyse the resulting telephone call and provide valuable coaching feedback on how the call was handled, what went well and how it could have been improved. Indeed, in advance of the call, AI may be able to provide suggestions on likely objections and how these can be handled most effectively. The ability to analyse and provide feedback on every aspect of the sales call from discovery, sales pitch, objection handling to sales closing will be very helpful in developing the skill of salespeople. We are already familiar with warnings that calls may be monitored for training and monitoring purposes and so I can see little challenge to this development in the future. It will be perfectly possible for AI to provide deep analysis of actual live sales calls if the salesperson wears special glasses providing both audio and video capture. I anticipate greater resistance to this from the Suspect but such tools will definitely be available very soon.

Chatbots will also be able to assist salespeople with tasks such as scheduling appointments, sending follow-up emails and answering routine customer questions which will save a great deal of time and improve productivity all round.

None of the above tools should replace the regular manager to salesperson monthly reviews but will provide the manager with the ability to provide a constant flow of developmental training to each member of the team and these tools will themselves provide additional input to the manager regarding specific and tailor-made training programmes for each individual in the sales team.

However, this book is about Sales Leadership and, I believe this will always be a distinctively human skill set. The original title of this book was Great Sales Management but I quickly realised that company culture has and continues to change away from a more directive style of management towards a more inclusive, leadership style. Today, people coming into the job market do not relate to the concept of a 'job for life' as their predecessors may have done. Instead, they see themselves as self-employed, prepared to contract their services to an organisation provided that the organisation meets their requirements on hygiene factors (pay and benefits) and, increasingly on what the organisation can do for them in terms of training and development as well as satisfying them with regard to their policies towards diversity and inclusion and sustainability. Such a sea-change has created a need for managers to incorporate the softer skills of coaching and develop their leadership capabilities.

This explains the explosion of the coaching industry over the last 20 years. As this trend develops, I am certain that students will be taught coaching and leadership skills at schools and into higher education. From a business perspective, there is a hard economic payback from the development of these more advanced leadership skills in terms of staff recruitment and retention and customer retention. The future for sales leaders looks very exciting with new tools to assist them in building a high-performance sales team. I will watch the evolution with great interest and make sure I keep up with the pace of change in my own coaching practice.

# RECOMMENDED READING

Mike Weinberg: *Sales Management.Simplified* (2016)
Harper Collins Leadership

Mike Weinberg: *Sales Truth* (2019)
Harper Collins Leadership

Mike Weinberg: *New Sales Simplified* (2013)
American Management Association

David Ventura & Phil Jesson:
*Top 10 Tips For Your Top 10 Customers* (2019)
New Generation Publishing

Claire Pedrick: *Simplifying Coaching* (2021)
Open International Publishing Ltd

Michael Bungay Stanier: *The Coaching Habit* (2016)
Box of Crayons Press

Ed Wal: *Solution Selling: The Strongman Process* (2016 )
PG Press

James Clear: *Atomic Habits* (2018)
Penguin Random House UK

THIS PROGRAMME
WILL INCREASE
YOUR SALES IN
**90** DAYS

# SALES
# ACCELERATOR
# PROGRAMME

If you want to give your sales revenues a
serious boost, why not buy the Sales Accelerator
Programme. The Programme is written for senior
sales leadership in business-to-business companies
with sales teams. Developed by award-winning
sales coach Steven Jenkins, the Programme is
based on 45 years of working with start-ups through
to corporates. It identifies the main reasons why
companies consistently fail to achieve their full
sales potential and explains how to overcome
these areas.

The 3-month programme involves...

- 10 recorded Masterclasses covering the key areas companies fail to achieve their optimal sales productivity

- A comprehensive Workbook containing the transcripts of the Masterclasses with notes sections

- An intensive one-hour one-on-one coaching programme over three months with Steven Jenkins to help tailor the learnings from the Masterclasses to the specific needs of the company.

The methods explained in the programme have been used by many companies and can deliver results well within the 3-month Programme.

It should be noted that only a 1% improvement in sales productivity will deliver £10,000 for every £1 million of sales revenue. Much of this will drop to the bottom line. This could be the best investment your company can make in delivering improved sales revenues.

**Programme costs £5000 plus VAT**

For more information visit https://stevenjenkinscoaching. co.uk/packages/

Or book a session with Steven Jenkins to discuss on

https://calendly.com/stevenjenkinscoaching/sales-accelerator-programme

# NOTES

# NOTES

# NOTES